Heal Our Land

Heal Our Land

Securing God's Blessing on America

Jimmy and Carol Owens

Foreword by
Jack W. Hayford

Fleming H. Revell
A Division of Baker Book House
Grand Rapids, Michigan 49516

Published by Fleming H. Revell
a division of Baker Book House Company
P.O. Box 6287, Grand Rapids, MI 49516-6287

Printed in the United States of America

Library of Congress Cataloging-in-Publication Data
Owens, Jimmy.
    Heal our land : securing God's blessing on America / Jimmy and
Carol Owens.
        p. cm.
    Includes bibliographical references.
    ISBN 0-8007-5629-0 (pbk.)
    1. Spiritual warfare. 2. United States—History—Religious aspects—Christianity. 3. United States—Church history—20th century.
I. Owens, Carol. II. Title.
BR526.O94 1997
243—dc21   97-688

We've been robbed.
Gradually at first. Stealthily.
While we slept, enemies crept in.
They've ransacked the house.
They've stolen our family album—
    Our heritage,
    Our history.
Our family treasures—
    Our inheritance,
    Our wealth.
They've kidnapped and brainwashed our children.
They've set the house on fire.
They are stealing our soul.
We are America.

Contents

Foreword

Jimmy and Carol Owens became my friends when we were college-age kids just beginning to learn the grace of God's love and power in our lives and the purpose of his call upon us. Since those days we remember with such holy joy and high happiness, we have often been partners in witnessing mighty workings of our almighty Father. What they write about here holds the keys to God's *mightiest* of workings: how he can, wants to, and will change entire nations . . . if we will accept our role.

For that condition to be met—"if My people . . . will humble themselves and pray"—most of us need new eyes to see and a hope that will overthrow obstacles to our vision. We have all been fed on futility by the tenor of our times, and it breeds a paralysis of hope. But the truth is that the church was born to answer to such hopeless moments. These can be our finest hours, if we're nourished by the truth that shatters the passivity that futility has bred.

The liberating power of God's revealed truth in his Word, and the rejoicing power of his re-echoed truth through Spirit-filled music, have been united through Jimmy and Carol's mission—*Heal Our Land*. By means of these dual tools—their music and their writing—there are many being freed unto faith that our nation can be healed! This book is the "writing" half of those tandem resources. I believe it is an apostolic order of book you have in hand—one meant to create vision.

It's apparent that this is what the apostle Paul had in mind when he wrote, "I ceaselessly pray for you . . . that the Father would give you the spirit of wisdom and revelation, that, knowing Him, your heart's eyes might see and understand the high hopes of His call to you!" (Eph. 1:15–18).

He prays three things: (1) for an enlightenment through the Father's gift of spiritual help—"wisdom and revelation"; (2) for an increased "knowing" of the Lord himself—"that, knowing Him" (that is, more of his own heart and nature, his love and purpose for us); and (3) for eyes that see "hope"—a hope that is energized by a captivating vision of the resurrection power of Christ and his power potential waiting to be expressed through his church (Eph. 1:19–23)!

The Holy Spirit who inspired those truths in the Holy Scriptures is igniting their firepower to hosts of God's people today. In nation after nation, futility and passivity are being shattered as faith and passion for intercessory prayer are being awakened. The Spirit of hope is seeking to show us there is still time to heal!

For too long, too many have been lulled to sleep by the notion that the Bible only predicts gloom and doom for "the last days." It's true, this old world has its problems and worse ones are coming. But that isn't the whole story in God's Word, because for these dark times there is also a simultaneous promise of two grand and glorious possibilities:

- an outpouring of the Holy Spirit, bringing fresh, springlike vitality to all who open to him (Acts 2:17–18; Joel 2:23–29); and

- an overflowing harvest of spiritual fruitfulness, attended by unlimited restoration through national and individual healing and recovery (note especially Joel 2:24–25).

This book is about those possibilities, and how they can be realized and released through us who will let our eyes be touched by the Spirit, that we may see the hope; that in this winter of our world's discontent, we may see the springtime of God's promise, "Ask the Lord for rain in the time of the latter rain, and [He] will make flashing clouds, and give them showers of rain . . ." (Zech. 10:1).

Jack W. Hayford

Preface

If My people who are called by My name will humble themselves, and pray and seek My face, and turn from their wicked ways, then I will hear from heaven, and will forgive their sin and heal their land.

2 Chronicles 7:14

Second Chronicles 7:14 is a treasure chest of revelation. In one short verse it gives us the simple but crucial conditions for getting God's attention and securing his intervention in our lives. Meeting these conditions will change us, and it will change our nation. *Heal Our Land* will show you how to implement these simple secrets and become a powerful intercessor for needy people and needy nations.

In intercessory prayer we stand between others and God, asking for favor or forgiveness on their behalf. Or we may stand between others and Satan, pleading for God's intervention and using spiritual weapons to secure their protection and deliverance.

True intercession, however, involves more than prayer; it involves our lives. Throughout the book, we will refer to that type of true intercession as "life intercession." Life intercession is what we do, in addition to praying, by standing between others and despair. It fulfills 2 Chronicles 7:14's crucial "companion" Scripture, Isaiah 58, which says that if we defend the oppressed, house the homeless, and feed the hungry, the Lord will hear our prayers, our national healing will appear, our darkness will pass, and we will rebuild the walls and streets to live in (see vv. 6–14).

Through prayer, God does mighty things we can't do, and *in* prayer, he shows us what we *must* do and then empowers us to do it. But it all begins on our knees.

You needn't be a marathon "pray-er" or attain superspiritual perfection before you begin, but the more you know, the more effective you will be. *Heal Our Land* can be used for personal study, a study with one prayer partner, or a group Bible study/prayer laboratory in which everyone learns and practices together. There are thirteen sections of questions and suggestions to give you food for thought, discussion, and intercession. Almost anyone can lead.

As you experiment and make discoveries in this laboratory, it will take you, one important step at a time, from the foundations of personal preparation to the courage and clamor of spiritual warfare. Each step will be an exciting, transforming experience that will provide you with vital cleansing, protection, and equipping for the work of serious, nation-changing intercession.

One final note before we begin. Although Jimmy and I (Carol) wrote this book together, I will be telling the story from my viewpoint to keep the material readable and clear. With that in mind, let's begin.

Introduction

From the air Northern Ireland looks green and lovely as our little group flies into Belfast, but on the ground things look gray and grim. The airport runway has been freshly bombed. The streets are lined with bomb-blasted buildings, graffiti covers the walls, and rolls of barbed wire seal off alleyways.

A bloody seven-year resurgence of "The Troubles" between the Catholic Irish Republican Army (IRA) and the Protestant Ulster Defense League (UDL) is in progress. British soldiers, a provocative presence patrolling the city, are beset by terrorists at every turn. We are virtually in a war zone.

Nevertheless, our troupe, including Pat Boone, a few other Americans, and twenty or more English singers, perseveres. Joined by a ninety-voice Belfast choir, we've come to present a powerful musical ministry calling for spiritual unity among Christians in this place where they seem more inclined to shoot at one another than to unite.

At our auditorium a shattered window marks the spot where a British soldier was shot to death on the previous day. The IRA terrorists obviously are not in the mood for unity, nor is the internationally known militant UDL pastor who invites us to leave town. We decide to stay anyway.

Before leaving America we had asked God for a specific Scripture to guide us and were convinced that he gave us Psalm 20:1–2: "The LORD hear thee in the day of trouble; the name of the God of Jacob defend thee; Send thee help from the sanctuary, and strengthen thee out of Zion" (KJV). With that assurance, we push on.

On the day of the presentation, the city is tense. Apprehensive but excited and determined, both Catholics and Protestants line up at the doors by the hundreds. Outside they are subjected to a body search. Inside they are watched by sharp-eyed armed soldiers. It is the first interfaith meeting of any kind since the recent Troubles began, and the government is taking every precaution.

The music starts. The audience responds tentatively at first. Then they begin to praise and worship. As they do, something stirs in the atmosphere. Many weep. Some go to their knees. The Holy Spirit moves and the love of God falls like a sweet rain.

As we pray, a priest comes forward and brokenly begs forgiveness from his Protestant brothers, who love Jesus as he does. With tears he beseeches God to forgive them all for their animosities and to shed his Spirit among them. Immediately Protestant pastors rush to pray with him and to repent of their own hatred.

The meeting breaks wide open. As priests, pastors, laypeople, and soldiers join hands and mingle their tears and prayers, renouncing ancient hatreds, one of the sponsors quietly draws the attention of my husband, Jimmy, to two men who are embracing and praying together. One is an IRA leader, and the other is an English major in full battle dress.

The police later tell us that during our time there, for the first time since the seven-year Troubles began, there was not a single reported act of political violence in the city.

Why? Because during this time not only Belfast Christians but our own church, the Church on the Way in Van Nuys, California, along with another small but powerful California church, were fasting and praying for Belfast as they had promised to do. They were "sending help from the sanctuary" (see Ps. 20:1–2). When we returned home we received a letter from a small group of zealous young Christian intercessors in Israel who had heard about our ministry in Belfast. The letter read, in part, "We were fasting and praying for you every day here in Zion." They were "strengthening us from Zion," another confirmation of our promise in Psalm 20.

Because of God's intervention in Northern Ireland, we became utterly convinced that he would move on behalf of any nation in response to determined prayer and fasting. From that conviction came our musicals on national intercession, which have raised thousands of intercessors worldwide.

We believe that as Christians continue to pray for their nations with understanding and perseverance, meeting God's conditions for answered prayer as laid out in 2 Chronicles 7:14, he will respond with national healing. He is only waiting to hear from people who care.

He will do it for America.

PART 1

To Save Our Soul

We sit by and watch the Barbarian, we tolerate him; in the long stretches of peace we are not afraid. We are tickled by his irreverence; his comic inversion of our old certitudes and our fixed creeds refreshes us; we laugh. But as we laugh we are watched by large and awful faces from beyond; and on these faces there is no smile.

Hilaire Belloc

1

The Soul of a Nation

America! America!
God mend thine every flaw,
Confirm thy soul in self-control
Thy liberty in law!

"America the Beautiful"
Katherine Lee Bates

We hear political rhetoric about the soul of our nation, and we ask, Do cities and nations have souls? If we accept the dictionary definition of *soul* as "the moral and emotional nature—the vital principle which moves and animates all life," the answer is yes. Certainly every city and country has a unique emotional and moral character that shapes its politics, its art, and its trade.

Then we ask, How does God respond to this animating moral character of a city or nation? It's a straightforward proposition: He protects and blesses a God-honoring nation and curses a sinful one (see Leviticus 26 and Deuteronomy 28). That doesn't always imply direct brimstone action from heaven, however. Sometimes God simply removes his protective covering from a nation he once shielded but which has become rebellious (see Isa. 4:5–6; 22:8). When God, rejected and offended, removes his protective hand, sin flourishes unrestrained until society degenerates to the point of self-destruction.

Sin Unrestrained

Consider the city of Los Angeles as fire boils from the thousands of buildings torched in a three-day siege of mob terror after the controversial decision in the Rodney King trial. Imagine the spectacle of thugs and thieves smashing everything in sight, scuttling away with looted goods, leaping and laughing in an orgy of destruction. For many hours the overwhelmed police force is nowhere in sight, and the populace is terrified and helpless.

Or consider the mind-boggling shock in Oklahoma City as the federal building blows apart one quiet morning. Who could have imagined a terrorist bombing in that benign national heartland? But there it is, and the people are defenseless as a thousand pounds of explosives pancake one floor onto another, smashing tiny day-school children along with more than a hundred helpless employees. And much of the world actually witnessed the detonation of a pipe bomb at the Olympic games in Atlanta, which sprayed more than a hundred victims with homemade shrapnel of nails, screws, and shards of glass, killing a lovely young mother.

Death and destruction are happening in America's workplaces and playgrounds. Public reaction is not only outrage but a new, disquieting awareness of vulnerability. The question has become, Where next? The old certitudes of safety are gone.

These events in California, Oklahoma, and Georgia are only three of the more dramatic examples in an accelerated outpouring of demonic violence and crime across America. Citizens are barricading themselves inside their homes, fearful in the face of sin unrestrained.

Nature Unleashed

Then there is the frightening possibility that without God's protective covering we are vulnerable to the dispassionate and awesome forces of nature. Picture that quiet early morning in January when thousands of California citizens were tossed from their beds as their homes were flung about by the heaving earth, like a rat in the mouth of a terrier. Timbers snapped, beams fell, masonry disintegrated, windows imploded. Many people died. Within seconds, hundreds lost everything for which they had worked a lifetime.

In the aftermath of this catastrophic earthquake in Northridge, California, a suburb of Los Angeles, a television newscaster interviewed a shaken survivor. "What did you think when the quake hit?" he asked the young woman. "I thought it was Armageddon," she replied. "I always knew it would start in L.A."

While her eschatology may be a bit fuzzy, she had a sharp insight into the soul of her community and "the vital principle which moves and animates" its life. That area of southern California is known as the pornography capital of the nation. She feared that because its moral nature was in rebellion against God, it was in imminent danger of judgment. As the earth undulated and people were crushed beneath buildings and falling freeways, she thought the time had come.

Not only in California, with its fires and floods and quakes and mudslides, but all around the nation we see an ominous increase of natural catastrophes. Even unflappable television newscasters are shaking their heads in astonishment at the unprecedented devastation of nature unleashed.

What is going on? Is God trying to deal with America's soul? Pat Robertson and other leaders observe that God is certainly trying to get our attention. If we don't listen, things will only go from bad to worse.

As our government progressively legalizes sin by saying, "Yes, we shall" where God has said, "Thou shalt not," we will find ourselves in ever deeper trouble as a nation. As our leaders seek solutions to momentous military and economic problems and at the same time legislate God out of our national life, they will find to their consternation that things aren't working out very well. As our citizens flagrantly parade in the streets, flaunting their mutiny against God, they are spitting into the wind and targeting our nation for destruction.

Who, we ask, has the answer to all this? And the answer is, The church has. We are not helpless victims; we can become an intercessory force that will turn the nation around.

Buffer Zone Builders and Gap Standers

There is a gentleman in our neighborhood who jogs every day, rain or shine. This man is *old*. He looks like one of those shriveled-up potatoes you find abandoned at the back of the vegetable bin. His version of jogging is the "Tim Conway shuffle"—feet barely moving, arms pumping like mad. But every day, he's out there in his running shorts and baseball cap, eyes on the ground, stringy legs moving out, one tiny step at a time.

Our young grandson, Ryan, observed this phenomenon each day for weeks as his mother drove him to school. Finally he reached a conclusion. "Mom," he said thoughtfully. "You know what? That man is my hero."

Ryan is right. That's the stuff heroes are made of. It's the stuff intercessors are made of, too: determination, perseverance, one tiny step at a time until the goal is reached and God's purposes are completed.

With determination we can help build spiritual buffer zones around our cities and nation to restrain evil in our government, immorality in our society, crime in our streets, and the encroachment of false religions and the occult in our communities. With determination we can help bring about a nation-changing spiritual renaissance, a radical revival in our churches, and an unprecedented spiritual awakening across our country.

If all Christians who are alarmed and outraged over the state of our nation will only learn what to do and how to do it, we can change things dramatically. For many of us the desire is there; all we need is some understanding and determination. This book will help provide the understanding. The determination must be ours.

Now imagine the reaction when, one serene summer evening on the edge of a small country town, just as the birds are settling down and the cicadas are tuning up, the local gasworks explodes. The spectacular blast sends families racing outside, where they find the eastern sky blazing like the sun. As they stand gaping, wondering what on earth is happening, one four-year-old boy immediately figures it out. Wild with excitement, he begins shouting, "Jesus is coming! Jesus is coming!" With shining eyes, outstretched arms, and guiltless heart, he runs as fast as he can go, straight toward the light.

If we all thought Jesus were coming right now, would our first impulse be to run toward the light or find a place to hide? If we have failed to build buffer zones of righteousness in our nation, if we have failed to defend her with our intercession, we will have a great deal for which to be ashamed. We hold the key to our nation's survival. When intercessors fail, judgment falls: "I looked in vain for anyone who would build again the wall of righteousness that guards the land, who could stand in the gap and defend you from my just attacks, but I found not one. And so the Lord God says: I will pour out my anger upon you; I will consume you with the fire of my wrath" (Ezek. 22:30–31 TLB). "Therefore have I poured out My indignation upon them . . . Their own way have I repaid by bringing it upon their own heads" (Ezek. 22:31 AB).

International teacher Derek Prince believes America is already coming under God's judgment. So does Dr. Bill Bright. Billy Graham says if God doesn't judge America, he will have to apologize to Sodom and Gomorrah. Nevertheless, all these great leaders believe God is still looking for intercessors to "stand in the gap" and stay his judgment so that a great revival may sweep the world and multitudes may find salvation before the final curtain falls.

The soul of our nation needs to be saved. Only changed hearts can really change our society. For people to be godly, they must first know God. For people to know God, they must first hear the gospel. The goal of intercession for the nation is not to beg an outraged God to withhold his wrath so that people may safely continue in sin. Rather it is to bring about and maintain conditions in our society that facilitate the propagation of the gospel until God's redemptive purposes are completed.

Getting It Done

To do the job, we must be aware of what is happening in our churches, schools, courts, and government.

We, the people, are still the deciding voice in America, but if we are not informed, we won't know who the good guys are and which rascals to throw out.

We *must* get involved. Intercession is not a cop-out that allows us to remain safely at home, praying, if God is calling us to carry the struggle for righteousness to the streets, the courts, or the political arena. When we don't do our part in the process of running our society, we get just what we deserve. When we don't set the standards and determine the game plan, we find ourselves operating under someone else's agenda. Then we have to dig out entrenched and determined opponents.

But our real enemies are not flesh and blood (see Eph. 6:12), and our weapons are not physical (see 2 Cor. 10:4). So before we step into the physical arena, we need to learn to fight the spiritual battle in prayer.

Intercessory prayer must initiate and then accompany our activism and evangelism. In prayer we receive strategy, armor, and air cover for our daily ground battles, and the weapons of wisdom, grace, and love with which to defeat our adversaries. Even if we begin praying only a few minutes a day, we can make a difference in America's future. So start like Ryan's jogging hero, simply doing as much as you can, just as you are.

Maybe right now you're having a hard time with problems of your own and feel you can't possibly take on the problems of the nation. That's like saying you don't have time to fight the fire in the kitchen because you need to clean the garage. Meeting God's conditions for effective intercession can bring God's blessing into your personal affairs while preparing you to bless the nation.

Be aware, however, that no matter how powerful and persistent our intercession, we won't always see immediate results. Sometimes it's a matter of two steps forward, one step back, or of standing with our fingers in the spiritual dike to keep evil from breaking through and inundating us all. But never think our prayers are not making an impact. Our influence has never been more crucial. If we persevere, we will progress and prevail. America has seldom needed her intercessors more.

2

Good News
and Bad News

America is like the country singer, his spangle-covered suit glittering in the spotlight, who said, "You see this suit? It cost me one thousand dollars. These alligator boots cost five hundred dollars. This hat was three hundred dollars. But underneath I've got on the raggediest underwear you ever saw!"

That's America, star-spangled on the outside but tarnished underneath. Still, we must admit, we look pretty good, so long as we remember the rule: Don't let 'em see your underwear.

Our supermarkets are a dazzling display of affluence. Most of us live in air-conditioned comfort and wear fabrics at which kings of the past would marvel. Although we are grappling with the problems of the homeless and the truly destitute, the majority of even our nonaffluent folks have food on their tables and television sets in their living rooms.

27

Militarily and economically we can still rattle our sabers and our moneybags and immediately get the world's attention.

Spiritually we look good, too. Although 90 percent of the world's clergy minister right here in this country to 5 percent of the world's population, we have sent more missionaries to evangelize the world than any other country. Most of our people profess to being religious, although a Gallup poll found essentially no difference between the behavior of the churched and that of the unchurched.

There is still human decency around, still vestiges of neighborliness, still some nationalistic camaraderie around the Fourth of July, with its fireworks, hot dogs, mom, and apple pie. But we have a worm in our apple pie—and holes in our national underwear.

A Better Past

A French visitor to early America, Alexis de Tocqueville, wrote prophetically, "America is great because she is good. But if she ever ceases to be good, she will cease to be great" (*Democracy in America*, 1835). Yes, America still *looks* good, but she is no longer *becoming* good. Forgetting her source of life, forsaking her protector, America is being eaten up by moral and spiritual decadence, and without the intervention of God she's heading for self-destruction. Sometimes Americans, even Christians, become so accustomed to this status quo that we lose track of a better past and lose our vision for a better future.

If you once took American history in school, it might be interesting to try it again. You probably wouldn't recognize it these days, though; it's all become politically correct. Our heroes are, by and large, gone. Their mo-

tives and morals have been slanderously demytholo-
gized by atheists and humanists, people with their own
destructive agendas. It's a real shame.

It's hard for people born before World War II to realize that there is now a generation who doesn't know
that America was founded as a Christian nation. But it
was.

Praying in the dark, cramped cabins of their groan-
ing little ships, the Pilgrims, and the Puritans after them,
suffered months on the pounding oceans specifically to
establish a haven for Christian freedom and to bring the
gospel to the natives on this continent.

These dreams were written into the charters of all the
original thirteen colonies. Their constitutions and laws
acknowledged God. They mandated scriptural education in the public schools. All colleges were Christ-cen-
tered. A Christian profession was a requirement for
holding public office. All this prompted de Tocqueville
to write, "America is a nation with the soul of a church."

In a burst of extravagant enthusiasm, historian
Richard Frothingham wrote in 1872, "The spirit which
actuated the United Colonies was as much from God as
the descent of the Holy Spirit on the Day of Pentecost,
and was introductory to something great and good to
mankind."[1]

When the bickering Constitutional Convention was
deadlocked in 1787, Benjamin Franklin called the assembly to daily prayer, and shortly the delegates came
up with the most remarkable document of government
the world had ever seen. But as John Adams, our second president, later warned, "Our constitution was
made only for a moral and religious people. It is wholly
inadequate to the government of any other."[2]

Adams was right. As America's people and her gov-
erning officials have grown increasingly immoral and
irreligious, many provisions of the Constitution and its

amendments have been twisted to destroy the rights they were meant to protect.

Order in the Court!

While they have recently made righteous and heroic decisions that have mended some serious problems, much damage has been done by the Supreme Court in the past. Although the Constitution says the Court cannot make laws, the justices have essentially done it anyway, simply by reinterpreting the Constitution and then determining the constitutionality of laws by these new interpretations. And since they have decided that the Bible, the only absolute, may not be used as a reference point in law, the law is now whatever the justices say it is. Neatly done.

In *The History of the Decline and Fall of the Roman Empire,* historian Edward Gibbon wrote, "The discretion of the judge is the first engine of tyranny." Justice Hugo Black said that the Court's power to hold laws unconstitutional was not given by the framers but was bestowed on the Court by the Court.[3] And Thomas Jefferson warned early on that for the Court to decide on the constitutionality of laws would amount to despotism.[4] In spite of these warnings, in 1962 the Court, by manipulating the Constitution, began a systematic undermining of America's essential spiritual foundations. They started with those most vulnerable to their influence: the schoolchildren.

Isn't that logical? If you want to destroy a nation, what better way to do it than either to kill its next generation (as in the days of both Jesus' and Moses' infancy as well as in the abortion madness of our times) or, barring that, to subvert its next generation of leaders while they are still young and vulnerable?[5] President Abraham Lincoln said, "The philosophy of the schoolroom today is the philosophy of government tomorrow." Adolph Hitler said, "Let me control the textbooks and I will control Germany."

The greatest censorship going on in our country today is in our public schools, where all traces of God and Christianity are being deleted from our history and public life, except to impugn the motives of the early missionaries. In D. James Kennedy's words, "Had it been done by an enemy it would be considered an act of war."

In 1962 the Supreme Court finally took the first giant step toward accomplishing in America what secular humanists had been trying to achieve since the time of the French Revolution and the ensuing "Enlightenment": They formally prohibited prayer in the public schools.[6] In 1963 they followed this step by prohibiting Bible reading and the recitation of the Lord's Prayer in schools.

In 1980 they banned the posting of the Ten Commandments in schools, because they are "plainly religious" and "may induce school children to read, meditate upon, perhaps to venerate and obey the commandments."[7] Pray tell, what dire consequences might arise if schoolchildren were induced to honor their fathers and mothers, stop stealing, fornicating, and killing each other?

In 1985 the Court declared unconstitutional even "periods of silence" for meditation and voluntary prayer.

The next step in this mind-set is that morality must not be taught in school, because it is religious. So when the "rights" of atheists to protect their schoolchildren from the "dangers" of religion were favored over the rights of the pro-God majority, our character-determining moral standards went down, and most of our other standards went down right along with them.

As a result, we now have a generation well-coached in "safe sex" but functionally illiterate "eighteen-year-olds getting diplomas they can't read,"[8] graduates ill-equipped to work at even a subsistence level in our society, much less make any meaningful contribution to it. This creates the despair that results in the epidemic of drugs, crime, and violence in our communities. This functionally illiterate generation includes nearly one half of our adult population.[9]

While it would be simplistic to blame all our ills on the Supreme Court and ignore a thousand other avenues the enemy has used to get at the soul of our nation, this surely is one of his crowning coups. And now we are reaping what we have sown: a rudderless generation without the knowledge of God, without absolutes, without hope, without respect for life.

Fuel for Your Intercessory Fire

We are on a precipitous downhill slide:

- Since 1962, the year prayer was taken out of our schools, the crime rate has risen by nearly 800 percent.
- One out of every 270 Americans is in jail, the highest rate in the world.
- In most cities, gang members outnumber and outgun all the city police forces combined.

If that doesn't scare you, it should.

With 5 percent of the world's population, we consume nearly 50 percent of the world's illegal drugs. Drug and alcohol abuse fuel our homeless population, which is between 21,600 and 40,000 every night in Los Angeles alone.[10]

America is the world's leading producer, consumer, and exporter of pornography. A new porno film is completed every fifteen minutes. In 1996 Americans spent more than eight billion dollars on pornographic materials and sex entertainments, an amount much larger than Hollywood's entire domestic box office receipts, and larger than all revenues generated by rock and country music recordings.[11] We are not only fouling our own nest but corrupting the entire world.

Homosexual practices have birthed the pestilence of AIDS that puts every one of us at risk of our lives. Now, some say that what people do in private is nobody else's business, but this is simply not true when their private practices endanger everyone. We are like a group of people out at sea in a small rowboat. Suddenly a man produces a large drill and begins to bore holes in the bottom of the boat under his seat. When the rest of us finally notice with alarm that the boat is filling with water, we protest loudly. Instead of stopping his dangerous activity, the man with the drill is indignant. "You can't tell me what to do," he announces. "It's my seat!" Then he calls the ACLU.

While we need to speak the truth in love, we *do* need to speak. Rampant immorality affects us all:

- One in five Americans is infected with an incurable sexually transmitted disease.
- Adultery has increased by 200 percent.
- The divorce rate is now at 50 percent.
- The percentage of single-parent homes has tripled.
- The illegitimate-birth rate is as high as 80 percent in some communities.
- Teenage suicide is up by 200 percent.
- Sexual abuse of children is up by 2,000 percent.

- One and a half million unwanted, unborn people are killed each year.

America is also over 5.3 trillion dollars in debt—that's $5,300,000,000,000. The bad news goes on . . . and the government can't figure out what to do about any of it.[12]

Can intercessors make a difference in this mess? They not only can, they are. Life intercessors are praying and acting and God is listening and moving. Exciting things, small and great, are happening everywhere. That's the good news. Let's look at it more closely.

God 'n the 'Hood

The principal had had it. He was fed up with the 150 vicious fights and thirty-eight arrests at his school over the previous years. Why couldn't he and his teachers and the police control a bunch of ten- to thirteen-year-old middle schoolers? Nobody was reaching the roots of the problem in this inner-city area. The government certainly hadn't shown up with any answers, so the principal decided to see what God could do. He turned to a nearby Vineyard church, whose people were starting to go out on the streets to serve the neighborhood (life intercession). They loved the kids and they were willing to get involved. The principal invited this innovative church, whose outreach pastor is Duncan Ragsdale, to start after-school youth clubs.

To determine the kids' interests, the church produced "impact assemblies" by networking with Crime Stoppers, Inner Cities for Jesus, and the Family Life Training Center. Youth with a Mission (YWAM) brought in an exciting allegorical dance-drama, *Toymaker and Son*. The kids were spellbound. After that they clamored to come to the club to learn drama and music, mime and dance, and athletics. They also learned more about Jesus. And they loved it all. The very next year, there was no trouble in the school—not a single fight!

When the other principals heard about it, they wanted in on the deal, too. As a result, within one month that year there were twenty-seven assemblies in thirteen schools, reaching more than nine thousand students.

One principal is a humanist, a black activist who loves her students and the people in the community. The church loaned her a musician to help with music teaching for her kids. Next they offered facilities for her teacher-training meetings. Then they hosted a luncheon for her teachers, during which a YWAM outreach team served tables and sang some songs from our musical *Heal Our Land*—the ones about racial reconciliation and care for the children. The teachers broke down and wept. They saw that this church had no hidden agenda of personal kingdom building. This is an outward ministry: Hit the streets, meet the needs, serve the people. It was right up their alley. Some of them received the Lord.

All this has had a tremendous impact. The ministry has grown from one church to a coalition of churches, now called Heights Outreach. It has such great rapport with the kids and teachers that the ministry leaders now help with tutoring and act as the school's truant officers, counseling and praying with absentee kids and their families. This year one school with a huge truancy rate had 988 kids with perfect or improved attendance out of 1,250 students.

This transformation in the schools has opened up the whole area to the gospel. The churches are now performing and witnessing in the parks and the malls. They are reaching homes and businesses everywhere. In their own neighborhoods, they are establishing "houses of prayer." They now have 100 such houses and are aiming for 1 for every 100 homes, a total of 250.[13]

The kids have a new vision, too. They're giving back to their communities and their schools by helping the poor and elderly, painting over graffiti in their neighborhoods, washing teachers' cars, handing out Thanksgiving turkeys, and serving Christmas breakfast to their schoolteachers.

Quite a metamorphosis, wouldn't you say? And all this in just over two years. It started with determined intercessory prayer.

The church began its life intercession using two vital spiritual principles: servanthood and networking. Not only did the church work with YWAM and others but, according to one pastor, much of the eagerness and availability of the people result from the influence of another ministry, Promise Keepers.

Promise Keepers, that great outreach to disciple and motivate Christian men, gives us more good news to report. It is growing exponentially, attracting more than seventy-two thousand men at one recent presentation and linking Christian men all across America. In 1996, 42,000 pastors gathered at a special Promise Keepers event in Atlanta.

There is widespread awakening and response to the dynamic of networking across the nation and the world. At the recent Mission America briefing in Chicago, the Southern Baptists enthusiastically put their enormous network of resources at the disposal of the body of Christ at large to finish the job of world evangelization. Shortly after, at a conference in Korea, they repeated that commitment. In fact, that conference drew unprecedented promises of cooperation and teamwork from major denominations and ministries worldwide to see closure of the Great Commission. Nothing of this magnitude and potential has ever been seen before. This is the church at its most exciting and effective.

How would you like to be part of a community-transforming network? How would you like to help your churches take responsibility for some of your community's problems and the needs of the disadvantaged? In every city there are many ongoing community development efforts that will be delighted to welcome you aboard. They are not hard to find if you're serious about looking for them. You can help them feed, clothe, and shelter hundreds of desperately needy people. You can help them provide health care and job training. You can help develop a new inner-city generation by assisting those who are ministering to gangs, or those who are providing quality education and biblical foundations to a multitude of almost hopelessly disadvantaged children. And as you do these things in the name of Jesus, you can help men and women find God.

If you truly want to become a prayer- and life-intercessor, plug into the Christian Community Development Association, founded by Dr. John Perkins. The association's second yearly conference was attended by nine thousand leaders involved in life intercession ministries nationwide, and its membership directory[14] is a resource guide of more than 450 contributing organizations. This marvelous network, through sharing ideas and experience, stays on the cutting edge of the most effective community-transforming ministry programs in America, as well as a few abroad. The network will tell you what is already happening in your area. It will also connect you with others across the nation to help your churches start new community-transforming coalitions and programs that *work*.

These kinds of cooperative efforts are producing some dramatic results. For instance, our friend LaVerne Campbell tells us that out of a coalition of suburban and inner-city pastors in Atlanta came an innovative housing program for the inner-city working poor that provides low-cost apartments and enables people to buy their own homes—a dream come true for many. From there the coalition began educational programs, job training, and placement services. LaVerne knew they had hit paydirt when one of the pastors reported that his large congregation had burned their last welfare card and that all his people were employed and housed! This program continues to help rebuild and revive the community. LaVerne and the other pastors will be glad to share their methods with you in detail.[15]

Another wonderful coalition is Mission America, with which our own Heal Our Land movement networks closely. It has many ministry facets. Its honorary chairmen are Dr. Billy Graham, Dr. Bill Bright, and Dr. John Perkins, and it includes almost every major evangelical denomination and Christian organization in the nation. Mission America is in the process of linking the churches in four thousand American communities to present the gospel to every person by the end of the century. Here, in an open letter by its chairman, Dr. Paul Cedar, past president of the Evangelical Free Church of America, are its goals and its enthusiastic recommendation of the Heal Our Land movement as a resource to achieve those goals:

> Mission America is a spiritual movement comprised of a growing number of ministry networks, churches, denominations, and parachurch ministries from across the nation. In a real sense Mission America is the response of a host of evangelical Christian leaders to the prompting of the Holy Spirit to cooperate and collaborate during the final five years of this millennium in the vital ministries of united prayer, revival/spiritual awakening, reconciliation, and world outreach.

What can we do together better than we can do separately to reach our community for Christ? This is a basic question of Mission America.

With this in mind I most enthusiastically recommend to you the ministry of Heal Our Land. This unique and powerful ministry begins with an interactive contemporary musical prayer meeting for America. It acts as a spiritual magnet to draw churches together and lead the people of God into transforming prayer and action that God can use to lay the foundation for true spiritual harvest. Heal Our Land is more than a one-time event. It includes follow-up seminars to motivate and equip the church for ongoing intercession, spiritual warfare, and Christian community involvement.

We encourage you to prayerfully consider presenting this powerful ministry tool as a united church outreach in your community. We believe that God can use it to impact churches, communities, and our entire nation to experience revival, spiritual awakening, and a great spiritual harvest in America and the world. That is our prayer!

The goal of the Heal Our Land movement is not only to motivate but to equip and enable intercessors who will bring revival to our churches and radically change our world.[16]

Start the Revival *Where?*

So where does this revival begin? In the inner cities, those melting pots of tongues and cultures and agendas, those seething hotbeds of rage and sin. That's where the coming great revival in America may well spring up.

If inner-city Christians recognize that they are of one blood—African American, Hispanic, Asian, Anglo, everybody—if they recognize and honor one another's spiritual gifts and legacies, they may plug into the most powerful spiritual force this nation has ever seen.

Already many African American churches, both urban and suburban, led by pastors with vision and courage, are changing the face and the heart of our cities. They are growing dramatically in numbers, grace, love, spiritual power, holiness, and dynamic community influence. We believe that in these and other "minority" churches, God is ordaining real revival for the nation. These churches deserve the prayer support and practical encouragement of every Christian in America. We also believe that God is gracing them with an "opposite spirit" whereby they offer love to those who have given them hate, healing to those who have wounded them. You just watch as God makes them a light to the nation, with healing in their wings!

But all these good things are only drops—growing and consequential drops, to be sure—in a vast and angry ocean of need. They are sterling examples of what a relatively few dedicated people can do. And they are only a glimpse of what God will do if his people refuse to sit back and let the devil devour their communities and their nation, but instead invoke God's sovereign power and undergird his outpouring by determined intercessory prayer and availability for life intercession.

Everywhere, intercession leaders are sounding the call and believers are rallying to the battle for rebuilding, awakening, and revival. They are spearheading a spiritual force—the praying church—that will ultimately determine the destiny of America and of the world.

These intercession leaders are turning people to God's ifs—his crucial requirements for answered prayer. These ifs have less to do with indignation at sin or with courage in spiritual warfare than with personal purity, actions, and attitudes, especially in relationship to God and to other people. Elementary as these conditions sound, this is where powerful prayer strategy begins. And that is the foundation for everything that follows.

God's ifs are neatly outlined in 2 Chronicles 7:14 and Isaiah 58. But before we consider them further in the following chapters, remember: You don't have to be an expert before you begin to pray! Right now you can turn to the suggestions and prayer list at the end of this book (appendix A), roll up your sleeves, and tackle this thing. However, just as the champion athlete must spend a lifetime in preparation for the moments of victory in competition, so God's ifs are the prayer warrior's vital, ongoing training. They are there to give progressive understanding, power, and protection and to help you pray with confidence.

Thinking It Over

1. How do you feel about the spiritual, moral, and economic climate in America? What cause and effect do you see among these three?

2. What characteristics do you see as the "soul" of your city? How do you think the soul of your city rates with God?

3. What do you see as the ultimate purpose of praying for the nation?

4. How do life intercession, evangelism, and intercessory prayer work together?

5. How do you feel about the efforts of some to remove God from our schools and national life? What can you do about it?

6. Take another look at the list of American social problems. Do you think the programs we've mentioned in this chapter would work in your community? Would you be willing to be involved?

7. How can you get your church involved in the problems of the needy in your community?

Suggestions for Prayer

- Pray for revelation of your personal gifts, callings, and responsibilities in the body of Christ.
- Pray for determination and perseverance to make national intercession an ongoing, habitual part of your life.
- Ask for wisdom and instruction for action on these moral, political, and spiritual issues we have discussed.
- Ask for direction for personal and church involvement with the disadvantaged in your community.
- Pray for the Supreme Court.

3

If *My* People . . .

For you are all sons [children] of God through faith in Christ Jesus.

Galatians 3:26

We are heirs of the Father,
We are joint heirs with the Son.
We are children of the Kingdom,
We are family, we are one!

"We Are Family"
Jimmy and Carol Owens

The Family: Getting It Together

The church is the people of God functioning together. Or not.

In our children's musical *Ants'hillvania*, one of the characters is a lady millipede. Onstage her voluminous skirts and petticoats cover several dancers who make up the parts of her segmented body and many legs. When life is smooth and undemanding, she dances along beautifully. But at the least challenge from an enemy, each pair of feet takes off in a different direction. Unable to get herself coordinated, she is left on the floor, disheveled and defeated, in a tangle of legs and white pantaloons. The church has the same problem. When we compete instead of cooperate, we become dysfunctional, a divided and ineffective force in the warfare for our nation's soul.

It's easy to ignore this failure on our own part and fix the blame for national conditions on "them": crooked politicians, greedy industrialists, grubby militants, and a large assortment of social misfits. "Lord," we coach piously, "straighten these people out so we can have a little peace and quiet in our society."

Amazingly, God isn't as concerned with straightening "them" out as he is with straightening out his own family. Only when he gets us into proper relationship to himself and to one another will we be unified and fit for him to use to turn the nation around. So before he can heal the land, he must start the healing, uniting work in us: "If My people who are called by My name . . ."[17]

Although we see a wonderful rising tide of unity in our land—ministry networks and powerful citywide pastors' coalitions forming across the country—united churches and ministries are still in the minority. Too often, "successful" ministries, which should be leading the way, become too "tunnel visioned" by an entrepreneurial mind-set. They fail to recognize that there are some things—such as evangelization of the world—better done together than alone, no matter how big they may be or how far they have reached. Unity—oneness of purpose—gives the church her credibility with the world. That's why Jesus prayed, "[I pray] that they all may be one, as You, Father, are in Me, and I in You; *that they also may be one in Us, that the world may believe that You sent Me*" (John 17:21, emphasis added). How tragic to see the church's potential power sacrificed on the altar of independence and self-sufficiency.

Satan has only to divide us to defeat us. He knows that no family divided against itself can stand and every kingdom divided against itself comes to ruin (see Matt. 12:25). He knows that united churches, moving in grace and love, generate a force—through agreeing prayer, spiritual warfare, and joint outreach—that even the gates of hell can't withstand.

Corporate love and unity in the church begin with individual relationships, and our attitude toward these things is determined by our point of view. Take, for example, the crotchety old man standing in a crowd watching a magnificent peacock display its tail feathers. As the bird's iridescent plumage flashes and shimmers in the sun, the peahens are properly smitten and the human observers are enchanted. The old man, however, is not impressed; his only comment about this moment of beauty is that the bird has the skinniest legs he's ever seen. We all might do better to focus on the good things in other people and just accept the skinny legs. It's not the answer to everything, of course, but it's a great beginning.[18]

"All right," you may say, "I'll try. But how do I make myself accept and love people who hurt me and make my life miserable? If love just isn't there, there's nothing I can do about it, right?" Yes, there is. The key word is *do.* Do love. We can do the thing that is most Christlike and benevolent, no matter how we feel. We can turn inward to the Holy Spirit for his reservoir of quiet answers and acts of blessing rather than dealing out our own snappy retorts or the well-deserved punch on the nose.

Often, however, no new point of view or anything else will heal an already damaged relationship, until we deal with the crucial issue of forgiveness.

I Beg Your Pardon

A bitter, depressed young woman came to us for prayer. Her problem? She was enraged at her husband's boss and coworkers, who were making his life and hers miserable, and she couldn't seem to change her attitude.

We asked her if she had ever confessed her resentment as sin and brought it to the cross. No, she answered, she'd never thought of it that way. Jimmy suggested she give all that hatred to Jesus as quickly as possible.

She immediately began to confess. She named them all: coworkers, relatives, neighbors. She had a list that sounded like the telephone directory. We listened in amazement, wondering how she had ever functioned under such a load of resentment.

When she finally finished, Jimmy led her in a childlike but profound prayer: "Lord, I bring this sin to your cross and ask your forgiveness. By faith I'm releasing all these people from my resentment. I'm putting this garbage in my heart into a big spiritual bag and giving it to you to carry out of my life forever. I know this is your will, and I'm trusting you, in your faithfulness and power, to do your part."

Then Jimmy prayed that for every person she had named, God would carry away her bitterness, bring love in its place, and give her peace. When he finished praying, Jimmy cautioned her that if her old thought patterns reemerged, she might have to think back to that night and reaffirm what she had accomplished there. Some things take time, he said. But when we saw her weeks later, she was glowing.

"You told me it might take time," she explained, "but it didn't! I was free that night and I've been free ever since."

"Oh, me of little faith," Jimmy muttered as we watched her walk away smiling and holding her head high.

Through unforgiveness our friend had put herself in a place of torment. She was like the servant in Jesus' story who, although forgiven a great debt by his king, had a fellow servant thrown into prison for his failure to pay an insignificant amount. As a result the king was outraged. "Wicked servant!" he cried. "Why couldn't you have had mercy on him just as I had on you?" The king then gave him over to the torturers until he paid all he owed (see Matt. 18:23–34). Now here's the scary part. Jesus said, "This is how my heavenly Father will treat each of you unless you forgive your brother from your heart" (v. 35 NIV).

How many Christians live in depression and spiritual defeat, not recognizing that they are tortured by a torment of their own making? If you feel angry, depressed, and distanced from God, it could be torment caused by unforgiveness. But you don't have to live this way. As you have brought the bondage on yourself, so you can set yourself free by an act of your own will. Confession, repentance, the cross; there is the answer.

Try the procedure Jimmy used:

- Lay it all out before the Lord.
- Confess it as sin and cast it all on him.
- Receive his forgiveness by faith.
- Be free!

Be humble enough to ask for help if you can't get victory by yourself. If you have uncontrollable anger or mood swings, get counseling. You'll find that you're not alone in this need and that people will be caring and supportive rather than shocked and condemning.

Willingness to forgive is absolutely critical for the intercessor. Jesus tells us not to bother coming to the altar if we are at odds with someone. Leave your offering, he said, and go make peace. Then come back to the altar—"the place to meet with God" (see Matt. 5:23–24). "Your heavenly Father will forgive you if you forgive those who sin against you; but if you refuse to forgive them, he will not forgive you" (Matt. 6:14–15 TLB).

How can we pray effectively if we harbor the sin of unforgiveness in our hearts? "If I regard iniquity in my heart, the Lord will not hear me" (Ps. 66:18 KJV). Our prayer offerings sit on the altar, waiting for us to forgive.

Building Intercessors: There's No Place like Home

No relationships are more crucial to our spiritual power than those in our own homes. And there is no place where forgiveness, new viewpoints, and "doing love" are more important, because when we are out of harmony at home, we feel out of harmony with God. Then our prayer lives suffer. You probably know the feeling. So how do we get things back on track?

Intercession can be a means of family restoration as we practice God's ifs. It also gives us a place of agreement and common focus, and this includes the kids. Children can become serious intercessors if we start them out on things that matter to them. It even works with independent teenagers! We "adopted" our kids' friends, many of them from dysfunctional homes. Without pinpointing their character flaws, we listened to their hearts, taught them to forgive, and helped them pray about their concerns. Soon they began to pray for one another. As they saw God answer, their faith soared, their prayer horizons expanded, and their lives were radically changed. That was years ago, but most of those young people are still walking with the Lord, and some are in ministry.

Today there is a multitude of potential young intercessors just waiting for encouragement and leadership. At a recent See You at the Pole day, when high school kids nationwide met at their school flagpoles for early-morning prayer, more than two million showed up. Out of twenty-four thousand secular schools in America, ten thousand have prayer clubs on campus, many the fruit of that day of corporate prayer.

Many children of YWAM families are veteran intercessors. One Easter their international King's Kids group was invited to perform on the Don Ho stage show in Honolulu. Glad for the opportunity to sing the gospel, they agreed. As they waited backstage to go on, the children, ranging in age from six to sixteen, broke into groups to pray. They pleaded with God to have mercy on the unsaved adult performers and melt their hearts.

After the show the adults, impressed by the kids' talent, surrounded them. The children told them about Jesus. Showgirls, wrapped in their dressing gowns, began to cry. One of them reached out to the children and said, "Oh, you're so clean and I'm so filthy. What should I do?" It was an evangelist's dream come true, and the children knew what to say and how to pray. They aren't little parrots, these kids. They pray and witness with faith born of experience.

For instance, while they were singing on the streets in one of the rawer districts of the city (under the watchful eyes of YWAM leadership), a crowd of prostitutes, addicts, and other such citizens gathered to listen. A transvestite approached Joshua, the six-year-old son of one of the leaders, and said mockingly, "Wouldn't you like to pray for *me?*" After asking his father's permission, little Joshua took the man's hand and prayed that Jesus would forgive his sins and save him. The man began to shake and scream, then sank to his knees on the sidewalk, crying out to God. Later a letter from the man arrived at the YWAM base, saying that he had indeed given his life to Christ on the street that night. He was cleaning up his lifestyle and making a fresh start. A little boy's simple faith and prayer power had changed everything for him.

Children will often pray with amazing tenacity and faith. But they must be taught—no, shown. And they have no better example than their parents. Give your kids a chance. Teach them the principles for effective intercession and then live them out yourself. It takes time and dedication, but it may be one of the most important commitments you'll ever make. As you do this, both you and your children can become powerful ambassadors for the kingdom of God in your daily lives.

A Kingdom: Ambassadors under Construction

In addition to being family, God's people are meant to be citizens, ambassadors, and bearers of the authority of Jesus' name:

> For he [the Father] has rescued us out of . . . Satan's kingdom and brought us into the kingdom of his dear Son.
>
> Colossians 1:13 TLB

> Now then we are ambassadors for Christ.
>
> 2 Corinthians 5:20 KJV

> He who believes in Me, the works that I do he will do also. . . . Whatever you ask in My name, that I will do, that the Father may be glorified in the Son.
>
> John 14:12–13

Understanding this is crucial to our spiritual strength and our power in intercession.

What does it all mean? How does it work? Picture a small girl of our acquaintance. She is only six but she is nobody's fool. She learned early how to use her father's name with authority—and with beautiful results. She keeps the local juvenile roughnecks in line by announcing, "Remember, my daddy is Frank Williams and he's a policeman!" Standing there with flushed cheeks and blazing eyes, small dimpled fists planted on her hips, she is confident and impressive. At least, she impresses the troublemakers, who clear the area in nothing flat. They have had previous dealings with her daddy. They understand the authority he represents and that he is both able and willing to deal with anybody who pesters his little girl. The fact that she stands small and alone against several ornery little boys doesn't faze her; she has complete confidence in the results she can achieve through her father's name. She never fails.

Jesus came to frustrate the devil's plans (see 1 John 3:8), and he has commissioned the church to do the same (see John 14:12). "Go in my name," he said, "and I am with you always" (see Matt. 28:19–20). Done with understanding, faith, and wisdom, invoking Jesus' name procures his overruling presence and power over Satan's kingdom.

However, Jesus' name is not a magic word to give us what we want, like a dime in a gum ball machine. It is meant to be used by mature and obedient people prepared to represent God's kingdom in our world. It is to be used to accomplish the will of God.

The church is the functional outpost of God's kingdom. The good news of the kingdom is this: Those who are bound by sin and Satan can be released. A more powerful kingdom than his has come, offering asylum and deliverance through us, Christ's ambassadors.

To do our job properly, we have to learn

- the extent of our authority and responsibility;
- the will of God as expressed in his Word;
- how to receive instructions through the discipline of prayer.

This book will supply some of this information for you. But God has supplied more than information; he has supplied a personal guide. The Holy Spirit was Jesus' guide and power source, and he must be ours.

The Spirit is the instrument or means by which we understand the things of God. If you were a scientist trying to convince a skeptical layman of the existence of microscopic life, you would be hard put to do it without a microscope. No matter how the other man might squint and strain, he wouldn't be able to see a thing. But once he has the proper instrument, a whole new world is opened up to him. Just so, the Holy Spirit is given to reveal the things of God to us. And he is the one who anoints and enables us. So whatever your understanding may be of how and when you received the Holy Spirit, be sure that you are filled with him now.

Get Back in the Pool

Every so often television will show an old film titled *Cocoon*. It takes place in a retirement home where the residents are finishing out their years in weakness and boredom. On their morning walk, three of the old gentlemen decide to investigate a mysterious deserted mansion next door. There they discover an indoor swimming pool. Soon they have acquired swim trunks and towels and are planning a break-in.

The men don't know that the pool contains large "cocoons," in which rest aliens, survivors of a spaceship crash. They are waiting for an interplanetary rescue team, and they exude an incredible amount of transferable energy. When the old men slip arthritically into the pool, they discover the cocoons. Finding them impossible to open, they decide to ignore them and go on with their swim. Within a few minutes they are leaping in and climbing out of the water like kids and swimming like dolphins. Later the other patients watch in amazement as their rejuvenated friends go out on the town for a night of break dancing. Soon their secret is out and everybody is in the pool.

Then—disaster. The house is boarded up. The pool is unavailable. Within a few days the old folks' energy fades and their joy disappears. The dancing feet begin to plod, the hands grow feeble and the knees weak. They are tired, discouraged, and powerless. They need to get back in the pool. And that's the rest of the story.

We are like that. Sometimes our spiritual lives, once so energetic and joyful, become mundane. Our dancing feet plod, our hands grow feeble and our knees weak. We need to plug into our power source. We need to get back in the pool.

The Bible says to "ever be filled [or ever be being filled] and stimulated with the Holy Spirit" (Eph. 5:18 AB). It says the disciples were filled and then refilled with the Spirit (see Acts chapters 2 and 4). We read that they were "continually filled throughout their souls with joy and the Holy Spirit" (Acts 13:52 AB).

The Spirit is God's great gift to the intercessor; he intercedes for us and helps us in our intercession (see Rom. 8:26–27). He shows us what to pray for and how to pray for it. Our job is to search the Scriptures, wait, and listen for his voice in our hearts. This takes time and perseverance, but it is the key to the heart of God and to making intercession he is eager to honor.

If you've never turned over control of your life to the Spirit, you can do it now. Open yourself up to God and ask him to fill you and keep filling you with himself. He has promised to do it (see Luke 11:11–13). Here's a short, simple prayer you can pray. We believe that if you pray it and mean it, God will honor it:

Holy Spirit, I yield myself to you. I invite you to take control of my very being. Teach me, anoint me, and use me for Jesus' sake. By faith I receive more and more of your life within me. I thank you for the precious gift of your living presence. Amen.

Thinking It Over

1. How might you help your pastor involve your church with other churches and ministries? What ministries might you work with, and what goals could you achieve?

2. If you attempted a cooperative prayer effort in your community, what response do you think you would get from church leadership? How might you approach such a project to get positive results?

3. Are you having difficulty with forgiveness? Are you willing to try something as childlike as Jimmy's method? Are you willing to ask for help?

4. How can you adjust your family schedule to accommodate regular intercession time together? How can you involve your children?

5. Is the idea of being an ambassador for Christ intimidating to you? Why?

6. Think about the role of the Holy Spirit in intercession. Are you willing to ask God for more of his Spirit? How do you think God will respond?

Suggestions for Prayer

- Pray for a fresh infilling of the Holy Spirit.
- Pray for unity in your church and among the spiritual leaders of your community.
- Ask for wisdom to help implement unified, corporate intercession.
- Ask for wisdom and perseverance to involve the whole family in intercession.
- Pray for the president's cabinet and other counselors.

Group leaders or study partners: Ask if some in your group (or your partner) would like to have prayer for personal needs such as salvation, family relationships, or church problems.

If My People Will Humble Themselves

> God sets Himself against the proud and haughty, but gives grace continually to the lowly (those who are humble enough to receive it).
>
> James 4:6 AB

> Pride goes before destruction and haughtiness before a fall.
>
> Proverbs 16:18 TLB

As a case in point, let me introduce you to Antony, the hero of our children's musical *Ants'hillvania*. Actually, Antony is the Prodigal Ant, son of the Command-ant of Ants'hillvania. Tired of working hard and living by the Wisdom from Above, he wants to be an Independ-ant. Full of arrogants and overconfid-ants, he leaves home to seek fame and fortune, singing as he goes:

I'm gonna be rich, I'm gonna be famous,
I'm gonna be dashing, I'm gonna be free!
I'm gonna be wise, I'm gonna be noble,
I'm gonna have power,
I'm gonna be *wonderful, beautiful, marvelous meee!*

Right from the start, everything goes wrong for Antony. After many hard knocks and close shaves, he returns home broke, bedraggled, and humbled—and with a new perspective on life. He has become a Repent-ant.

His little "Independ-ant's Song" not only reveals Antony's character but may reveal our own as it addresses some ramifications of God's first big *if* for answered intercession: humility.

"I'm Gonna Be Rich!"

Being rich sounds great at first, doesn't it? But love of money corrodes our values, warps our perspective, and messes up our spirits. Americans, even Christians, are especially prone to use money as a gauge of personal value and a source of pride, an ungodly and destructive standard.

I remember the day Mary Lou stopped coming to church. Usually as dependable as Old Faithful, suddenly she was missing from her job in Sunday school. And she never came back.

One day we met her on the street. Reluctantly she answered our questions about her absence.

"I'm sorry," she said, "but I just can't handle it anymore."

"What do you mean?" we asked.

"Bill is out of work," she explained. "We don't have any money."

We were puzzled. "What does that have to do with not coming to church?"

She began to cry. "There's just nothing left over after we pay the rent and buy food. I can't help it about our clothes."

It seems she overheard several "pillars of the church" gossiping in the ladies' room. They were criticizing the way she and her children dressed, and agreed that the hard-up little family was definitely lowering the image of the place. They cut her to the heart.

In contrast, God tells us not to be snobbish but to be happy with humble tasks and humble people (see Rom. 12:3, 10, 16). Money is a power tool. In the hands of the righteous, it is a constructive marvel. In the hands of the immature and self-indulgent, it is disastrous. Not only can it make us snobs, it can make us Independ-ants, too. After all, when things are looking good, who needs God? When that happens, our prayer life disintegrates.

It's a problem saints and nations have struggled with for centuries:

> The love of worldly possessions is a sort of birdlime which entangles the soul and prevents it from flying to God.
>
> Augustine of Hippo

> Beware that in your plenty you don't forget the Lord your God. . . . For when you have become full and pros-perous . . . that is the time to watch out that you don't become proud.
>
> Deuteronomy 8:11–14 TLB

> Intoxicated with unbroken success, we [Americans] have become too self-sufficient to feel the necessity of redeeming and preserving grace, too proud to pray to the God that made us.
>
> Abraham Lincoln

Take a moment for a "heart check" by asking yourself a few honest, soul-searching questions:

- Have material goals become the focus of my life?
- Have the fruits of success dulled my appetite for the things of God?
- Where is my heart? For where my treasure is, there will my heart be, also (see Matt. 6:21). If what I treasure most is material, my heart will be earthbound.
- Have I fallen for the advertising hype? Am I spending more money on grown-up toys and status symbols than I am on feeding the hungry and bringing the gospel to a miserable, lost world?

If God has prospered you, ask him why. Prosperous Christians are meant to be the enabling hand of those who minister. Giving is both a spiritual gift and an office in the body of Christ (see Rom. 12:4–8). To miss God's purpose for prosperity is to lose it all. It takes only a stock market plunge, a disabling disease or, of course, death, and our material treasures are gone in a flash. All of them. Forever. In the end, only what we have done for the kingdom of God will go with us.

"I'm Gonna Be Wise!"

Our friend Jim Spillman was a respected associate pastor and educator in one of the largest churches in the United States. Intellectual Christianity was his forte and a source of pride. When he learned that a famous healing evangelist—without a single degree—had been invited to the church, he was appalled. He pronounced all such evangelists "frauds who hypnotize poor yokels who haven't been to school."

During the meetings he refused to sit on the platform. Instead he sulked in the sound booth high in the balcony, watching people below claim their healing. "Psychosomatic," he growled, "or phony." His stomach ulcers, sympathetic to his moods, began to hurt. Then when a staff member excitedly claimed that his deformed hand had been healed, Jim stepped out of the sound booth for a closer look. As he did, he was electrified to hear the evangelist announce, "A man in the balcony has just been healed of ulcers. Where are you? Come on down here."

To Jim's horror, the pain in his stomach vanished. As he looked for an escape route, a small soft-spoken lady, the evangelist's assistant, touched him gently on the arm. "You're the one, aren't you?" she whispered. Unwilling to admit it but unable to lie, he ground his teeth and nodded. With that the sweet little lady yanked him from his refuge, dragged him triumphantly to the railing, and with a voice like a trombone whooped, "Yoo-hoo! Here he is!"

Every head in the church swiveled in his direction. He was trapped, humbled . . . and healed. He had just added a degree in the sovereignty of God to his M.A. In that one evening Jim's spiritual perspective changed. He saw that no matter how well educated he was, he was a child to God and he had a lot to learn. So have the rest of us. If we really want the heart and mind of God as intercessors, we will have to lay down our own wisdom and intellectualism and humble ourselves like the simplest children:

> I thank thee, O Father, Lord of heaven and earth, that thou hast hid these things from the wise and prudent, and hast revealed them unto babes.
>
> Luke 10:21 KJV

I tell you, whoever does not accept the kingdom of God like a child will never enter it.

Mark 10:15 NEB

God has chosen "what in the world is foolish to put the wise to shame . . . that no mortal man should have pretense for glorying and boast in the presence of God" (1 Cor. 1:27, 29 AB). God reveals his heart to the most unlikely: the meek and the humble. As one astute preacher, a Scotsman, observed, "Have ya not noticed that God has the most disconcerrrting way of blessing the wrrrong people?"

"Beautiful Me!"

Black is beautiful. So are brown and white and yellow and red. God created us all as we are, and we are right to feel good about it. However, when racial pride becomes racial arrogance, we are headed for serious trouble.

For generations, racial and cultural arrogance have been a fact of life in our country, and now our chickens are coming home to roost. From the forcible subjugation of one race or culture by another in the past to the slurs, snubs, and injustices inflicted in the present, we have inherited some of the most serious and seemingly unsolvable problems in our nation.

But are they really unsolvable? Isn't the church the place where the healing of long-festering wounds should start? Isn't it the logical place for humility, repentance, forgiveness, and new beginnings? The place for intercession? The place to heal our land?

In the aftermath of that hot summer when racial outrage and violence exploded over the verdicts in the Rodney King trial, central Los Angeles was devastated. The job of cleaning up and beginning again was daunting. Where to start and what to start with? Everything was burned down or broken up. With most of the stores destroyed, there was nowhere to buy even such basics as food and clothing, assuming people had any money with which to buy them. Things were bleak.

Then, while buildings were still smoldering, the church appeared on the scene. These were life intercessors who came from everywhere, with truckloads of provisions. They offered cleanup, food, comfort, counsel, and conciliation. They represented nearly every racial, ethnic, and denominational stripe you can imagine.

Through an existing multiracial coalition of pastors and their churches called Love L.A., they were already prepared to help in such a crisis. They had been interceding together for months, seeking racial reconciliation. The love of Jesus touched the ravaged city through their compassion and ministry.

The multicultural, multiracial church of Jesus Christ holds our greatest hope for peace in America. But it begins with setting aside racial preconceptions and recognizing that all Christians have one Father and all are related by the blood of Jesus. Our relationship is spiritual, eternal, and real. It calls for acceptance and honor, respect and courtesy, equality and justice, between all God's people.

That sounds fairly easy. In reality, as Love L.A. understands, reconciliation requires a lot of humility . . . and some urgent fence-mending.

At the Southern Baptist Convention not long ago, those in attendance voted officially to label the years of black slavery and the ensuing years of discrimination by their own denomination as a sin. That has a lot of serious implications for them and their forebears. They formally and publicly repented for the church's history of bigotry and begged the pardon of the black community in America. This was a milestone step for them—humbling, crucial, and righteous.

Recently the Lutherans also publicly confessed, repented, and apologized for Martin Luther's malignant anti-Semitism, drawing great appreciation from the Jewish community.

Then, at a Christian convention in Holland, eight hundred Germans came before the other European Christians to confess, repent, and seek forgiveness for the unspeakable sins committed under Hitler. The others not only forgave them but pronounced a Year of Jubilee for Germany, a time of liberation from guilt and sorrow, a time for beginning again.

John Dawson's Reconciliation Coalition has been a strong voice in the United States, ministering to the wounds of Native Americans and African Americans on behalf of the church and earning a rave review in a front-page article in the *Los Angeles Times* in the process.

These are major acts of fence mending. They fulfill the first vital act of reconciliation: repentance for past and present wrongs. (This may apply to nonwhite bigotry, too. Some of us may have children who belong to gangs that regularly target other minorities—just for the fun of it or perhaps because of hatred they've heard expressed at home.)

All intercessors should repent, first for themselves and then for the church, which long ago should have led society from bigotry into love. Instead it has historically been guilty of virulent racism. But as you can see, things are changing dramatically.

Following the righteous lead of the Southern Baptists, we too can confess and repent for the racial sins of our forefathers. Many of us have ancestors who took part in stripping American Indians of their rights and land and leaving them with broken treaties and broken lives. Or ancestors who kidnapped black people and tore apart their families and hearts at American slave auctions. Perhaps some of us have had to deal with arrogant racial attitudes handed down through the generations and into our own hearts. We may say, "We had nothing to do with that; *we* would never have done those things. Why should we identify with our forefathers' sins? Is that even scriptural?" A legitimate question. Here's what Jesus had to say about it to Israel:

> Woe to you . . . (hypocrites)! For you . . . [say], "If we had lived in the days of our forefathers, *we* would not have aided them in shedding the blood of the prophets." Thus you are testifying against yourselves that you are the descendants of those who murdered the prophets.
>
> Matthew 23:29–31 AB, emphasis added

> I will send you prophets, and wise men . . . you will kill some by crucifixion . . . so that *you* will become guilty of all the blood of murdered godly men from righteous Abel to Zechariah (son of Barachiah), slain by you in the Temple between the altar and the sanctuary. Yes, all the accumulated judgment of the centuries shall break upon the heads of this very generation.
>
> Matthew 23:34–36 TLB, emphasis added

The Old Testament patriarchs often confessed and repented of the sins of their forefathers. We believe this "identification praying" is scriptural. (See "Daniel's Pattern" in chapter 8.) However, God allows us to repent on their behalf only after making sure our own hearts are clean so that given the chance, we truly would never commit the same sins as they.

Those of us who have been wounded may find that God requires some hard and humbling things of us too. He may ask us to forgive our enemies before we receive apologies or restitution. Why? Because it's God's way: *"While we were yet sinners,* Christ died for us" (Rom. 5:8 KJV, emphasis added). Love and the offer of reconciliation come from an offended God before repentance comes from the sinner. God asks us to operate in the ways of his Spirit rather than in hatred and revenge. It's called grace.

Prayer of Repentance and Reconciliation

Heavenly Father, we recognize that as believers we are one blood, one family, and one kingdom. We come in all humility, and on behalf of ourselves, our forefathers, and the church, we confess our poisonous sins of racial arrogance and hatred. We repent, Lord, and apologize to you and to one another. We have grieved your heart, wounded your people, and divided our churches and our society. In Jesus' name, forgive us.

Those of us who have been wounded ask for the supernatural grace to truly love and pray for those who have persecuted us; to forgive those who have despitefully used us, to show that we are the children of our Father who is in heaven (see Matt. 5:44–48).

Give us open hearts and hands and homes, to faithfully minister to the disadvantaged, to search for ways to bind up the lingering spiritual wounds and societal wrongs of the past. Father, from this time forward we pledge to treat all people with justice, dignity, respect, and benevolence, that the world may see the people of Jesus Christ first loving one another and then loving the whole lost world that Jesus loves and died to save. Amen.

5

What Can I Say After I've Said I'm Sorry?

There is an old song that asks the question, What can I say after I've said I'm sorry? Then it goes on to ask, What can I do to prove I'm sorry? Prayer is only a part of the repentance and intercession process. The process requires more than an apology and a few tears. There is life intercession to be done.

Healing Old Wounds

When our son, Buddy, asked a Native-American Christian leader what the white church can do to bring reconciliation, he advised these things:

- *Admit* the wrong. Many gross injustices have never been addressed or confessed. Surely the time is now.
- *Apologize* sincerely.
- *Ask* for forgiveness.

- *Ask* how to help.
- *Listen* to the answers!
- *Do* whatever is possible to make things better.
- *Pledge* loyalty, affection, and fellowship.
- *Honor* the pledge.

Real repentance, or change of heart, requires humility, courage, and honesty.

To bring healing to our inner cities, we have some practical suggestions for those who may be part of the middle- to upper-class Christian community: Change your lifestyle, adopt a mission, and practice life intercession.

Change Your Lifestyle

Change your lifestyle to release you financially to help care for the poor; to bring not only food and clothing but training and education to those who will receive it; to truly help the underprivileged achieve a better quality of life; to bring the gospel in all its ramifications right to where they live.

For example, John Beckett, a businessman and a friend of ours, has turned one of his factories into Advent Industries, a nonprofit organization that trains folks who have been labeled unemployable, most of them from inner-city environments. They are paid minimum wage as they are taught marketable work skills, basic educational skills, and the practical application of biblical principles, all of which builds positive social and work ethics into their lives. When the trainees are ready, the factory supervisor gets on the phone and places them in jobs. They have been at this for sixteen years, and more than 90 percent of their graduates are regularly employed.

Advent Ministries is a practical, no-kidding demonstration of the love of God. This kind of life intercession requires a new dedication and focus. It requires sacrificial giving, intercessory prayer, and hands-on involvement. (See the resources section of this book for information on starting this kind of ministry in your community. Contact Mr. Ed Padley.)

Adopt a Mission

Adopting a mission results in a strong involvement between suburban churches and inner-city missions. These missions are run by full-time life intercessors, people with God's heart who are struggling to do an overwhelming job with the homeless and hungry while most of us are not even aware—or don't care—that they exist. These life intercessors are on the streets in the midst of danger and death to *show* the gospel, the message that God loves every person in every strata of society and cares about each one personally. They are the love of God "with skin on."

And they are doing our hard work, our dirty work, for us. But the job is too big now for these few. We are just as responsible as they to minister to the crying needs in our own back yards. Again, we need to be available with our money and our very own personal helping hands and our persevering prayer. We need to find those home missions in our cities and ask them what they need, then help them pray until they get it.

You may be amazed at how God will move when you intercede for what is so close to his compassionate heart. For example, our friend Rich Boyer is on the board of directors of an inner-city mission that desperately needed a new facility. Since the board members had promised God never to build anything they didn't have cash to pay for, they had the work done in increments, paying for each part as they went along. Just as the end was in sight and they were making plans to move in, the builder told them that there was an additional thirty thousand dollars due immediately for unforeseen expenses. It was an honest mistake but a drastic one, because until the subcontractors were paid off in cash, the ministry couldn't move in. The board members were hit with the news on a Friday, and those subcontractors would be lining up with their hands out on Monday.

What to do? They brainstormed to try to come up with ideas for what they could trade, sell, or take out of their personal accounts to raise the cash, but there was no way they could get so much so soon. Then they realized they had neglected to pray. So pray they did—big-time prayers! At last, still out of ideas but resting in God, they went home to bed.

Bright and early Monday morning, a worker at the mission called them. "Please, get right down here," she asked them urgently. "This can't wait. I don't know what to do." They went to the mission as quickly as they could.

"I found this box on the front steps," the worker said, presenting them with a heavy, brown, unmarked package. She had found it sitting right there, out in the open, in the worst part of the city. "No note of any kind," she went on. "It can't possibly belong to us, can it?" The mysterious box held silver bars, antique gold coins, and gold Krugerrands (coins from the Republic of South Africa).

The board members called the police, who told them to hold the stuff until they checked for reported thefts. Several hours later they called back: No thefts had been reported; the treasure now belonged to the mission. The board members called a collector of coins and precious metals who appraised, and bought, the contents for $30,056.

Practice Life Intercession

Life intercession is involvement at a practical and loving level that will change our society gradually yet profoundly. Along with our fasting and prayer, it is what real intercession is all about. It will help keep our cities from exploding and give our witness credibility. It is right and righteous and we need to get involved quickly.

Although we need to be involved individually whether or not others respond, these things are most successfully done as a cooperative outreach by the church. This won't happen without pastoral leadership. There is something vital here that preachers need to be teaching and modeling to their people. James 1:27 says that pure and undefiled religion is taking care of the widows and orphans and keeping our lives uncorrupted by the world. Jesus said that at the judgment he will separate the people according to whether they have fed the poor, housed the homeless, clothed the naked, and visited the sick and the prisoners (see Matt. 25:31–46). He said, "When you refused to help the least of these my brothers, you were refusing help to me" (v. 45 TLB). Judgment will be meted out accordingly.

We don't know what this does to your doctrine, but it certainly shows what is important to the heart of God.

"Marvelous Me!"

There is one last, small item on Antony's pride list from the previous chapter that we just can't overlook: spiritual pride. This is a destructive disease that infects laypeople and clergy alike. For instance, veteran intercessors who are able to pray for hours at a time must be careful that their accomplishments, won over years of discipline and practice, don't make them feel superior to those of us who don't do what they do. Sometimes challenging people to Olympian feats of intercession only discourages them. Often the response is, "Oh well, if that's what I have to achieve, I'll never in the world be able to do it," and they give up right there. Intercession leaders should teach, demonstrate, and encourage but never intimidate (see 1 Peter 5:1–6).

Sometimes when God uses us to teach or help others, the temptation is to think, I must be pretty special if God is using me. I do believe I have arrived! When we reach this lofty position, we become the body's pain in the neck. From there we harden into doctrinal and theological molds. You know the attitude: I know all about it; my mind is made up. Please do not confuse me with the facts. At this point revelation may cease, and in time we may become what A. W. Tozer so aptly calls "staid guardians of sterile orthodoxy."

What all of us journeying souls in the pews long for are compassionate spiritual leaders who are living examples of love and humility. Humility is so important in intercession and spiritual warfare that we will mention it in several contexts throughout the book. Just as it was for Adam and Eve, pride has been the downfall of many a man and woman of God by keeping them independent and overconfident and therefore vulnerable to the enemy.

Thinking It Over

1. Why do you feel God puts such an emphasis on the attitudes of human pride and humility?

2. How might you and your church have a part in racial and cultural healing in your city?

3. As times become tighter economically, do you think God may require some changes in the thinking and

lifestyles of American Christians? How might that affect you personally?

4. How do you honestly feel about racial and social exclusivism—in clubs, organizations, work opportunities, housing, and so on? Can Christians righteously subscribe to such exclusivism? If so, to what extent? Can exclusivism be justified biblically?

5. How do you think the intellect and the spirit are different from one another? How are they meant to work together?

6. What do you see as some of the dangers of spiritual pride?

Suggestions for Prayer

- Pray for revelation of any prideful attitude in your life. Confess it and ask God's forgiveness.

- Repent for sins of racial discrimination on your own behalf and on behalf of your forefathers. You may use the prayer at the end of chapter 4.

- Ask God for revelation as to how you can help make restitution for these sins and heal the wounds they have caused. Ask also for a giving heart.

- Pray that God would use you to make a difference in your church, your community, and your nation.

- Ask God to use your church to make a difference in the nation.

6

If My People Will Pray and Seek My Face

Be eager for more frequent gatherings of thanksgiving to God and His glory, for when you meet thus, the forces of Satan are annulled and his destructive power is canceled in the concord of your faith.

Ignatius of Antioch

Thanksgiving and Praise: The Gateway to Intercession

It's true: Satan's destructive power is canceled by thanksgiving and praise. And it doesn't have to take place in a corporate prayer meeting. For instance, when a hurricane devastated parts of Florida and Louisiana, the television news showed people wandering around in a state of shock. Their houses and automobiles were piles of rubble, and they had no food or water. They were thankful to be alive, but despairing about the future. Every worldly

73

possession was gone. "There's nothing left," they cried. "What in the world will we do?"

One lady featured in the report had a different attitude. As she shoveled debris out of the shell that once had been her home, she said, "It will be all right. Something *good* will come out of it. He [God] will bring something good out of it yet." And she said it with a smile.

This lady understood and honored the character and ways of God, who works all things together for good to those who love him and who are called according to his purpose (see Rom. 8:28). No hurricane could make her change her mind or her testimony. Her words and her smile were a defeat for Satan, who would have loved to use this natural disaster to make her unbelieving and bitter.

As this lady demonstrated, thanksgiving and praise are more than emotional acts, they are choices—acts of the will in obedience and faith. They are proclamations of the good news that God is triumphant in every circumstance and over all the works of the devil. These proclamations of faith immediately stand us in the place of victory and usher us into the place of intercession: "Enter into His gates with thanksgiving, and into His courts with praise" (Ps. 100:4).

That the One who created galaxies without number and the cosmos of atomic structure would consider any of us worthy of notice is a manifestation of grace beyond any ability to express. Yet often people treat him as though he exists to serve them, as if he is a sort of heavenly butler who obediently fills their requests and who then should be grateful for a nod or a smile of acknowledgment. Great intercessors know better. They are invariably fervent thanks-givers who know that God manifests himself where he is praised (see Ps. 22:3).

Praise and thanksgiving are dynamic faith-builders that fix our focus on our marvelous, almighty, overruling God, who has all the answers and who is on our side. That's why the patriarchs often began their prayers with a long litany of the works of God, reciting his miracles of creation and deliverance. By the time they got through with all that, their faith was red hot.

Most veteran intercessors take literally the psalmist's simple advice: "Praise the Lord! Praise the Lord!" They lay down their inhibitions and openly speak their love to God. They have found this the key to his courts. There, as they delight in him, he answers their prayers (see Ps. 37:4).

You may say, "I'm not accustomed to openly expressing praise to God. I think I'd feel awkward, even in private. But I think this is right and I want to learn how." Let King David help you. Find a quiet place and read some praise psalms aloud to God. Then continue speaking thanksgiving to God, using your own words. Or try singing to him. Jimmy and I sing simple choruses during our individual worship times when nobody can hear us but God—well, usually.

I was alone in the bedroom one day having a good out-loud praise time, when Jimmy came rushing in, wild-eyed. "What's wrong? What's wrong?" he demanded.

"What do you mean, 'What's wrong?'" I asked indignantly. "There's nothing *wrong;* I was singing!"

"Oh," he said, looking embarrassed. "I just came to help. I thought somebody was crying."

So much for my vocal ability. But my heart was right and that's what counts.

At our house we have a motley collection of old valentines: made by hand, crooked, paste-smeared, misspelled, and funny. We wouldn't trade them for anything because our kids made them. They were gifts of love and they delighted us. We know the Father receives our stammering expressions of love in that same spirit of

75

delight. He doesn't want it to be perfect; he just wants it to be from us.

For us, thanksgiving and praise are a logical and important progression in intercession. They help us "come boldly to the very throne of God and stay there to receive his mercy and to find grace to help us in our times of need" (Heb. 4:16 TLB). They give us space between the nitty-gritty of everyday life and the change of spiritual venue we need as we seek God's face in worship.

Three Faces of God

Let's examine three specific but different faces of the awesome God we seek to worship: Monarch, Husband, Father.

Monarch

Our Creator-God is a magnificent monarch who doesn't need our vote to retain his office or our approval to ratify his actions. The prophets and apostles fell before him like dead men. They were not afraid of punishment; they were simply afraid of *him*. He is like a wild, unpredictable force of electricity that we are unable to touch and still live. But in Jesus he has given us a "transformer" who makes him available and touchable to us. He waits expectantly for our response to his loving availability.

"Now we may walk right into the very Holy of Holies where God is, because of the blood of Jesus. This is the fresh, new, life-giving way which Christ has opened up for us by tearing the curtain—his human body—to let us into the holy presence of God. . . . Let us go right in, to God himself, with true hearts fully trusting him to receive us" (Heb. 10:19–20, 22 TLB).

Husband

Worship—seeking God's face—is the place of intimacy. It is the place for expressing and receiving love, as a bride gives and receives love from her husband:

> For your Maker is your husband—the LORD Almighty is his name—the Holy One of Israel is your Redeemer; he is called the God of all the earth.
>
> Isaiah 54:5 NIV

> By law a married woman is bound to her husband as long as he is alive, but if her husband dies, she is released from the law of marriage. . . . So, my brothers, you also died to the law through the body of Christ, that you might belong to another [husband], to him who was raised from the dead, in order that we might bear fruit to God.
>
> Romans 7:2, 4 NIV

It is the place where fruit bearing begins. From the power of this personal, active, intimate relationship with our Lord, his character and works begin to grow out of us as naturally as a child grows out of the mother's womb or as fruit grows from the tree that gives it life.

Jesus longs for this relationship, for the passion of his bride's first love. For instance, after he acknowledges the toil, endurance, and spiritual discernment of the church at Ephesus, he says: "But I have this one charge to make against you: that you have left (abandoned) the love that you had at first—you have deserted me, your first love. Remember then from what heights you have fallen" (Rev. 2:4–5 AB).

In God's order of priorities the love relationship is the "height" of our life with Christ. The miracle, the wonder, is that he so freely offers himself to us as we seek his face. Again, he awaits our response to his availability.

Father

In this personal, one-on-one place with the Father, we receive balm for our wounds, comfort for heartbreaks, strength for our spirits, and instruction and discipline for maturity.

Zechariah was one such mature son—proven and trustworthy. God gave him a vision of angelic transactions before his throne. There God said to him, "If you will walk in My ways and keep My charge, then also you shall rule My house and have charge of My courts, and I will give you access to My presence and places to walk among these who stand here" (Zech. 3:7 AB). To grown-up, trusted sons and daughters today, the Father offers privileges and authority that perhaps we are only beginning to understand.

All of this revelation of the intimate faces of God happens in the Holy Place of God's presence. We need to find our way here, where we are changed, cleansed, and prepared for ministry and intercession.

Much as we would like to have this happen instantly, that is not the way it works. It's a process that will go on until we get to heaven, and it involves an old-fashioned method—personal repentance—as we see, once again, in 2 Chronicles 7:14: "If My people who are called by My name will humble themselves, and pray and seek My face, and turn from their wicked ways, then I will hear from heaven, and will forgive their sin and heal their land."

Repentance is one of God's required ifs, and it opens the gateway to intercession, where we see the face of God and receive healing for ourselves . . . and for our nation.

7

If My People Will Turn from Their Wicked Ways

If our consciences (our hearts) do not accuse us, if they do not make us feel guilty and condemn us, we have confidence (complete assurance and boldness) before God; And we receive from Him whatever we ask.

1 John 3:21–22 AB

If I regard iniquity in my heart, the Lord will not hear me.

Psalm 66:18 KJV

Repent: to reconsider; to think differently. To turn from a past course of action.

One at a Time

Sitting in our living room is Dawn, a throwback to the hippie lifestyle, all love, peace, and granola. She knows nothing about Christian ethics or morals; she only knows that Jesus has just come into her life and that with all her heart she wants to please him. She has a question: "Is there anything wrong with my living with my boyfriend and having sex with him?" she asks with wide-eyed innocence. "I mean, like, does it bother God?"

As we try to frame a tactful but true answer, she goes on. "See, I don't know what the Bible says about it, but I've been feeling very uncomfortable about it myself, and I wasn't sure what I should do."

"Oh," we say, "well . . ."

"So," she says earnestly, "I kicked him out. And it really took a load off."

The Holy Spirit has done his job without any help from us, thanks, because he has found what he's looking for—honesty and a heart hot for holiness.

On the other hand, we have an unsaved and unhappy acquaintance who is also a fairly successful businessman. He cheats his clients—not a lot, just enough to keep the profit margin healthy. It's the way his close-knit little company does business. He knows that if he wants a relationship with God, he'll have to take a new stand where he is or find a new job and new friends. Although it's driving him crazy, he just won't do it. The cost is too high. So he lives on in frustration, his heart torn, unable to enjoy what he's working so hard to achieve—and risking his soul in the process (see Mark 8:36).

Like many people, our friend doesn't see that repentance isn't meant to be a heavy, onerous duty; it's a marvelous privilege of grace, a doorway to spiritual freedom and joy. God isn't waiting to beat up on us as we confess and turn from our sins, but to forgive, refresh and renew us, and purify us for service.

Jesus says that before any of us can take a speck out of another's eye, we need to take the log out of our own (see Luke 6:42). Before the church can be effective in intercession for secular society, we need to confess our individual and corporate failures and beg God's pardon. God is out to purify the church—one of us at a time. He's after our characters. He's after our relationships with families, friends, sweethearts, and business associates. All he needs from us are willing hearts.

All Together Now . . .

Individual repentance and renewal is what makes us a holy and powerful church. Purity is the source of our credibility.

Picture a beautiful fall morning in a large city. The convention center is overflowing with people who have come to hear some of the best-known Christian speakers in America analyze the troubled state of the nation. As they rail against pornographers, abortionists, and homosexual activists, the crowd—myself included—stands and cheers. Yes, we agree, in order to clean up the country, we must do something about this unrighteous bunch now!

However, some things bother me. While most of the speakers carefully direct their hatred at the sin and not the sinner, some are vitriolic; some are sarcastic and insulting. I wonder, How would I feel if I were a homosexual feeling disturbed about my lifestyle, or a pornography addict wondering if I could ever be set free, or a pro-choice advocate having doubts about my stand on abortion? Might I not be reluctant to come to these people for help? Might I not feel that Jesus Christ, whom they profess to represent, also looks on me with scorn and revulsion? And might I not wonder if they are really as righteous as they seem to think they are?

Mulling over these attitudes, I leave the auditorium for the snack booth in the foyer. On my way I greet the security guard at the door. Then I walk to the booth, buy my food, and return by the same door. To my surprise, the guard now asks to see my ticket.

"But you just saw me walk out of here," I say.

"I know," she replies. "Show me your ticket anyway."

As I juggle my food and dig out my ticket, an observant usher politely asks the guard why she has made me go to all this trouble.

"Okay, I'll tell you," she says. "A lady from your crowd did the same thing at the last break. She walks up and talks to me, then goes out to the foyer. There she goes up to a waiting friend and gives her ticket to this other woman. Then she goes to the snack booth, buys some food, and comes back through my door, smiling and chatting like an old pal. I say, 'Let me see your ticket.'

"'Why, you know me,' she says, acting surprised and put-out. 'You just saw me go out right through this door.'

"'Right,' I say. 'Let me see your ticket.'"

Then the guard finishes. "I don't know whether she thought I was blind or stupid, but believe me, she didn't get in."

As I hand over my ticket, I wonder what that guard thinks about a Christian woman so busily condemning others while blatantly hatching her clever plot to defraud the convention sponsors.

Involving ourselves with the big, objective issues, such as prayer for the sins of the nation, can make us feel wonderfully righteous. Concentrating on other people's sins gives us a beautiful opportunity to ignore our own. But national revival and cleansing has to begin with us, the church.

Frankly, in recent years we've seen enough sin going on in the church to make us wonder if Christians still believe that God means what he says about how we are to live. We've all been shocked by the big, media-circus cases involving sexual indiscretions and various frauds perpetrated under the guise of religion. But these are only the public cases.

Take an acquaintance of ours, for instance, who runs a large, ministry-related business. He happily admits to us, "I *love* to wheel and deal. I love to win! And I'll take you if I can." He isn't kidding. He retains a battery of lawyers to protect him from litigation by people he has "taken" and to sue other Christian businesses when that seems profitable, even though God forbids us to sue one another (see 1 Cor. 6:1–11).

In one independent evangelical church, another acquaintance is on the ministry staff, although he's living with his fourth wife, having divorced all his previous wives—leaving each for the next—even though God condemns adultery.

The church's image is at an all-time low. Unchurched people watch the television news and see pastors shooting abortionists, and heavily armed militants parading around carrying crosses, threatening to kill police officers and government officials. They see ministers and priests accused of fornication and child molestation. They think this is really Christianity. No wonder they laugh at religion. Worse, they laugh at Jesus. "Born again" has become a term of derision.

The world may not want to be pure, but it respects purity. The tragedy is that it doesn't see it more often in us. We can change this situation. We can confess and repent of our personal sins, all those things we've swept under the rug and tried to ignore. Then we can repent on behalf of the church, just as we repented for the sins of our forefathers. (See "Daniel's Pattern" in chapter 8 for more information.)

Repenting Individually and for the Church

There's no time like the present to take care of neglected housecleaning. Take a few quiet minutes to look deep inside. Ask the Holy Spirit to begin the convicting process, then listen. Soon things will come to mind: the unforsaken secret sins, that bad-news love relationship, those delightful but ungodly friends who are influencing your lifestyle, the unethical business practices. Those are the things that have to go. Sometimes they are hard to get rid of, but confession, repentance, and the cross are still the answer.

You might pray like this:

Father in heaven, I am yours. I love and worship you. Knowing and pleasing you are my eternal concerns. All other concerns I give to you— my relationships, my fortunes, and my future. I want my ambitions and character to conform to your plan for me. Forgive my sins. [Take your time here and name them.] *I bring them all to the cross to be paid for by Jesus' sacrifice there. Cleanse me now for Jesus' sake. Now, by faith in your promise, I receive your forgiveness and cleansing. Amen.*

Once you have done this kind of praying from the heart, don't keep beating yourself by repeatedly confessing and repenting of sins already put under Jesus' blood, forgiven and forsaken. This trivializes and insults his work on the cross. Of course, if you are having difficulty breaking habitual sins or walking through deep repentance, by all means go to your pastor or spiritual counselor for help. They will help you find forgiveness and freedom.

Once we have cleaned up our own hearts, we're ready to repent on behalf of the church and pray for her revival. To help you identify some failures of the church and make a thorough confession, here are some suggested prayer excerpts from the *Heal Our Land* praise and prayer presentation. You may cover all these issues in one session or concentrate on one at a time for intensive meditation and prayer. However you do it, don't rush through it; set yourself for some serious intercessory work.

Father in heaven, as we grieve over the wickedness and degradation of our nation, we recognize that it is partly because of our failures as your church that our society is as we see it now.

Because we have tolerated impurity in the church, our witness has been crippled. Because of our silence, the voices of sin and rebellion have grown clamorous in our nation. Because of our apathy, we have injustice in our courts and crime in our streets. Because of our divisions, we have been too spiritually weak to stop the inroads of the devil.

Forgive us, Lord. Forgive us for the doctrinal pettiness and squabbling that have presented an ugly, fragmented picture of Christ to a world longing for spiritual reality and love. Unite us so the world may see you in us and believe.

Where we have become powerless by trusting in our own programs, resources, and traditions instead of being led by your Spirit, where we have compartmentalized religion to a few hours a week instead of making you the motivating force of our lives, where we've become idolaters by putting other things before you, forgive us.

Forgive us for tolerating evil and becoming friends of the world, compromising our high and holy calling. Because of our reluctance to offend the world with our protests, we have pornography available in our living rooms, heresy and perversion taught in our schoolrooms, and the slaughter of the unborn in our public clinics.

It is time for judgment to begin at the house of God. But we want to judge ourselves so we will not be judged by you. So hear our confession, Lord, and restore to us all we've lost through our sin. Make us hungry for your Word and powerful in prayer. Help us to abandon everything that offends you. Wake all your people to the ministry of prayer and fasting for our nation, with authority and confidence and power.

Let us again be salt and light in our corrupt and darkened world. Let righteousness and holiness preserve us, our churches, and our nation. Amen.

Thinking It Over

1. How do thanksgiving, praise, and worship prepare you for intercessory prayer?

2. Do you see the connection between your spiritual fruitfulness and your intimate worship relationship with the Lord?

3. If you aren't accustomed to expressive worship, are you willing to stretch your comfort zone a bit and try it in your private devotions? If you've already started, how has it affected your spiritual life and your relationship with God?

4. How do you feel about your privilege of direct access to the presence of God? Do you think your personal response to that privilege has been all it should be? What needs to change?

5. What happens to us in the Holy Place? How does it lead us to repentance?

6. How does the world react to our self-righteousness? Is this justified? What should we do about it?

7. Why is our personal and corporate repentance so crucial to the future of our nation?

Suggestions for Prayer

- Thanksgiving: Name your blessings, especially as Americans, and express your wholehearted gratitude for them.
- Praise: Acknowledge and praise God for all his wonderful works of creation and redemption. Sing to him. Read psalms to him.
- Worship: Forget your self-consciousness and focus on his presence in your midst (see Matt. 18:20). Declare aloud his divinity, power, and majesty. Acknowledge that he is Lord above all lords, powers, authorities, and names that exist. Tell him that you love him.
- Pray for the president and his family.

PART 2

Praying for the Nation

Can plunder be taken from warriors, or captives rescued from the fierce? But this is what the LORD says: "Yes, captives will be taken from warriors, and plunder retrieved from the fierce; I will contend with those who contend with you, and your children I will save."

Isaiah 49:24–25 NIV

8

Then I Will Hear from Heaven and Heal Their Land

For the kingship and the kingdom are the Lord's, and He is the ruler over the nations.

Psalm 22:28 AB

It is a fateful day in the Philippines. The Catholic church has finally taken an official stand against the oppressive Marcos regime, and things are happening fast: the people take to the streets, President Marcos calls out the troops, and the revolution is on.

Soon the revolutionaries take over the main radio station and begin playing Jimmy's "If My People Will Pray" anthem at regular intervals around the clock. It becomes the theme song of the struggle. The people sing it as they go, unarmed, to face the troops.

Grim and menacing, tanks growl through the streets of Manila. Reaching the human barricade, they pause. It is the perfect scenario for a Tien-anmen Square–style slaughter. But miraculously, face-to-face with their fellow citizens, the soldiers refuse to fire. Soon many climb down from their tanks and join the crowd. With that, it is all over. God, always in ultimate control, sovereignly gives the people a bloodless victory.

The action in the streets is not simply the result of long-seething anger on the part of secular citizenry. It is the fruit of long seasons of fervent, persevering prayer and fasting by laypeople and clergy (hence their devotion to our song), and the courageous stand for righteousness by priests and pastors. When the time finally was right, God moved dramatically in response to their intercession.

Later we see a taped speech made by President Aquino at an all-night prayer rally featuring the *If My People* musical, presented by the Filipinos. She exhorts the people to serve Christ for the good of the nation. Like an evangelist, she finishes with the motto, "Jesus Christ is Lord of the Philippines and of all nations!"

Mrs. Aquino, knowing that God is sovereign and that nations carry within themselves the seeds of his blessing or judgment, urges her people to serve him and thus build a "wall of righteousness" to protect the destiny of the Philippines. Their response will determine their future.

Let's Make a Deal

God is in control, and he blesses or chastises the nations depending upon their response to his lordship. Obedience will get them the best deal possible:

> All these blessings will come upon you and accompany you if you obey the LORD your God: You will be blessed in the city and blessed in the country. . . . [Your] enemies

. . . will be defeated. . . . The LORD will grant you abundant prosperity—in the fruit of your womb, the young of your livestock and the crops of your ground. . . . The LORD will . . . send rain on your land in season and . . . bless all the work of your hands. You will lend to many nations but will borrow from none. The LORD will make you the head, not the tail.

Deuteronomy 28:2–3, 7, 11–13 NIV

Then God drops the other shoe. The curses for disobedience are the most awful list of calamities you can imagine. Here they are, greatly condensed and without the lurid details of incurable sores, siege, and cannibalism. First, though, he reverses all the aforementioned blessings. Then he adds:

If you do not obey the LORD your God and do not carefully follow all his commands and decrees I am giving you today, all these curses will come upon you and overtake you: . . . [Your] sons and daughters . . . will go into captivity. . . . The alien who lives among you will rise above you higher and higher, but you will sink lower and lower. . . . Because you did not serve the LORD your God joyfully and gladly in the time of prosperity, therefore in hunger and thirst, in nakedness and dire poverty, you will serve the enemies the LORD sends against you. . . . The LORD will also bring on you every kind of sickness and disaster . . . until you are destroyed. . . . Then the LORD will scatter you among all nations. . . . There the LORD will give you an anxious mind, eyes weary with longing, and a despairing heart. You will live in constant suspense, filled with dread both night and day, never sure of your life.

Deuteronomy 28:15, 41, 43, 47–48, 61, 64–66 NIV

We realize that no other nation has the same covenant relationship that Israel has with God. Nevertheless,

God's principles of blessing and cursing apply across the board. The Old Testament is full of his warnings to heathen nations as well as to Israel. However, he always leaves room for a national change of heart, as when he sent Jonah to cry doom to Nineveh, then spared them when they repented. God can and does play hardball in dealing with governments. He uses them either to bless or to chastise the people—or both.

Let My People Go

Imagine three-month-old baby Moses bobbing gently in his little basket among the reeds of the Nile, seemingly abandoned to the whims of chance. The next thing you know, he's an Egyptian prince. Then he's a slave. Then he's a revolutionary waging a titanic power struggle with Pharaoh—whose heart is hardened by God—for the freedom of the enslaved Israelites. God has orchestrated this whole complex political chronicle for two reasons: to reveal his power and lordship to Egypt (see Exod. 14:18) and to bring faith and the fear of the Lord to Israel (see v. 31).

Then look at God's careful maneuvering to put these people into positions of political power: Joseph in Egypt, Esther in Persia, Daniel in Babylon. All of them rise from slavery to rulership in idolatrous nations. There they become instruments through which God delivers his chastised people.

There is no government anywhere that God has not put in power (see Rom. 13:1). Daniel 4:32 says that God rules over the kingdom of humankind and gives that kingdom to whomever he wills to govern it. For example, God sovereignly removes Shebna, the wicked steward of Judah, saying, "[I] will hurl you away violently . . . into a large country. . . . I will thrust you from your office, and . . . will call My servant, Eliakim. . . . I will clothe him with your robe . . . and will commit your authority to his hand" (Isa. 22:17–21 AB). God raises up and pulls down to suit his own plan.

Even Pilate, the heathen governor of Judea, is put in his place of authority by the will of God. Although he seems to be the deciding voice in Jesus' fate, Jesus tells him flatly, "You would not have any power or authority whatsoever against (over) Me if it were not given you from above" (John 19:11 AB).

Jesus' death is the centerpiece of God's greatest deliverance plan of all. So he does not interfere as Satan sets up Jesus' betrayal through Judas or as the ruling Jews, fearing Jesus' influence with the people, demand his crucifixion or as Pilate, fearing the Jewish leaders, sends Jesus to his death. It is a hotbed of mixed motivations, fueled by fear and ambition and fanned by Satan. And God has coordinated it all.

Although he isn't aware of the implications, Caiphas, the high priest, has it right when he prophesies to the worried members of the Sanhedrin: "Being the high priest that year, he prophesied that Jesus was to die for the nation, And not only for the nation but also for the purpose of uniting into one body the children of God who have been scattered far and wide. So from that day on they . . . plotted together how they might put Him to death" (John 11:51–53 AB).

It is a divine sting operation: By allowing Satan to manipulate these influential people and bring about Jesus' death, God has watched him busily orchestrate his own doom. If the satanic rulers and powers had known God's plan, "they would not have crucified the Lord of glory" (1 Cor. 2:8). Satan envisioned only Jesus' death; the resurrection and ascension never entered his mind.

Take Asa, for Example

To see how God responds to wise and righteous governmental leadership, let's look at Asa, the king of Judah. As Asa rides home from battle, Azariah the prophet runs out to meet him.

"Listen to me," Azariah shouts as he delivers this simple corollary of God's justice. "The Lord will stay with you as long as you stay with him. But if you forsake him, he will forsake you." He warns the king that if the nation rebels against God, God will plague them with trouble. There will be civil war and international war, and crime will flourish. They will eat the fruit of their own sin.

Asa believes the prophet. He takes crucial action that not only keeps Judah out of trouble but sets a significant example for us: He leads the people in fervent repentance (see 2 Chron. 15:1–15).

First Corinthians 10:11 says that the things that happened to our spiritual forefathers are illustrations of the way God works and are written down as examples for us. Certainly, if our nation continues in rebellion, we will eat the fruit of our sin, too. Perhaps the solution to our problem is the same as theirs.

What do you suppose would happen in the United States if our president emulated the king of Judah and led the nation in repentance? True, he might be either impeached or committed. Or on the other hand, under the moving of God, the people actually might repent, and our nation might be delivered from destruction. It has happened before.

Abraham Lincoln understood that when nations forget God, they reap judgment. He also understood that repentance and intercession bring mercy. He saw the biblical precedent of national leadership setting the example and sounding the call. Three times he issued proclamations for "A National Day of Humiliation, Fasting and Prayer." The proclamation for April 30, 1863, read in part:

> . . . we know that by His divine law, nations, like individuals, are subject to punishments in this world, may we not justly fear that the calamity of civil war which desolates the land may be but a punishment inflicted upon us for our presumptuous sins, to the needful end of our national reformation as a whole people? We have been the recipients of the choicest bounties of heaven. . . . We have grown in numbers, wealth, and power as no other nation has ever grown. But we have forgotten God. We have forgotten the gracious hand which preserved us in peace, and multiplied, enriched and strengthened us; and we have vainly imagined . . . that all these blessings were produced by some superior wisdom and virtue of our own. Intoxicated with unbroken success, we have become too self sufficient to feel the necessity of redeeming and preserving grace, too proud to pray to the God that made us! It behooves us, then, to humble ourselves before the offended Power, to confess our national sins, and to pray for clemency and forgiveness.

Mr. Lincoln called for a day "holy to the Lord," dedicated to fasting and intercession as the people suspended their normal pursuits and gathered in their churches and homes to seek God. His speech went on:

> . . . in the hope authorized by the Divine teachings, that the united cry of the Nation will be heard on high and answered with blessings, pardon of our national sins, and restoration of our now divided and suffering country, to its former happy condition of unity and peace.

If ever a national leader had a clear revelation of what was necessary to heal his land, this man had.

While it would be the most effective and exciting thing imaginable to have this kind of spiritual leadership from our president, the church can't afford to wait for it. We have already had our call to repentance and intercession from the Head of another kingdom.

Daniel's Pattern: Identifying with the Sins of the Nation

Picture our three-year-old son, Buddy, running for cover at warp speed. He has been very naughty and I am running after him with the flyswatter. As I finally corner him, I give him one swat and take aim for another. Of course, he begins to cry. At this point Jamie, his five-year-old sister, rushes to his rescue. With a pleading look at me, she stands between us and takes him in her arms. "Poor little guy," she croons as he snuffles on her shoulder. She stands in the gap, loving him, knowing her own little backside is in jeopardy. Of course, the disciplinary session is over. It is a clear-cut case of successful, single-handed intercession.

Just so, though in a serious and desperate situation, Aaron the high priest runs into the midst of the rebellious congregation of Israel as God begins to pour out the discipline of death: "For there is wrath gone out from the Lord; the plague has begun!" (Num. 16:46 AB). Holding a censer of fire and incense, a symbol of prayer, he makes atonement for them: "And he stood between the dead and the living, and the plague was stayed" (v. 48 AB). Just as it was part of Aaron's priestly duty, intercession is also a part of the church's duty as "priests unto God" (see Rev. 1:6; 5:10).

The problem is the same today as it has been for centuries: The nations need to repent but, with a few historical exceptions, do not. So God, in his mercy and love, listens for intercessors. Through them the fate of nations can be changed. Without them judgment will fall. It has been the same throughout history.

Remember for a moment Moses, trembling and alone, standing between his guilt-laden people and a furious and dangerous God. Or Nehemiah, weeping, mourning, and fasting for days for the restoration of his decimated nation. And then there is Daniel, an ongoing one-man prayer meeting. No one has ever given us a more powerful pattern for intercession for a nation than he has. Chapters 9 and 10 of Daniel are outstanding examples of the effectiveness of the intercession of one righteous man.

Daniel's prayers were effective because he came with determination and humility: "I set my face to the Lord God to make request by prayer and supplications, with fasting, sackcloth, and ashes" (Dan. 9:3). And he prayed the right kind of prayers. Young's Bible Concordance defines the word used for *pray* in 2 Chronicles 7:14 in this way: "to judge self, to pray habitually." These two principles were vital to the success of Daniel's intercession:

1. He judged himself first. He confessed his own sins, not claiming any personal goodness but throwing himself on the goodness of God for deliverance.
2. He prayed habitually. Daniel didn't wait for days of desperation to sharpen up his prayer life; he was a prayer warrior with a disciplined spirit. And he persevered until he heard from heaven.

Daniel's intercessory method was to name the specific sins of his nation and of the national leadership, confessing and repenting of them as if they were his own: "O Lord, to *us* belong confusion and shame of face—to our kings, to our princes, and to our fathers—because *we* have sinned against You" (Dan. 9:8 AB, emphasis added).

Nehemiah also used this method, identifying himself with the sins of both his nation and his forefathers when he prayed: "Let Your ear now be attentive and Your eyes open to listen to the prayer of Your servant which I pray before You day and night for the Israelites, Your servants, confessing the sins of the Israelites which *we* have sinned against You. Yes, *I and my father's house* have sinned" (Neh. 1:6 AB, emphasis added).

Daniel's and Nehemiah's kind of "identification praying" brings dramatic results. Jesus, of course, is the greatest possible example, as he identified himself with the sins of a lost world and "stood in the gap" between them and the judgment of God.

Our nation, too, desperately needs faithful, persevering intercessors who will name her sins and repent of them on behalf of the people. Tragically, we have a bountiful harvest from which to choose. We might start by naming the things that brought destruction to Sodom—which were not only idolatry and blatant homosexuality, as we tend to suppose, but pride, idleness, and too much food, while the poor and needy suffered unnoticed (see Ezek. 16:49–50). And of course, like Daniel, we need to pray fervently for our leaders.

As we will see in the following chapter, we will do this most successfully when we know how God wants us to pray for the people with the power.

9

Praying for the People with the Power

The missionary's file is open on the desk of the minister of religion as the missionary enters the office. Although the missionary had been given permission to broadcast the Christian gospel in this Muslim nation, which wants to project the image of religious freedom to the world, it seems he may have become too successful. The government suddenly has questions about his message and motivations.

Before discussing the file, however, the official offers refreshments, saying, "We Muslims have a custom when we are visiting with friends; we share food with them."

The missionary replies courteously, "We Christians have a custom when we share food with our friends; we ask God's blessing on it. May I pray?"

The Power of Positive Prayer

The missionary prays fervently and lovingly for the nation, asking God to protect the president and other officials and to make them righteous and wise. The minister of religion is astounded to hear a Christian pray in this way for his country. "I do it every single day," the missionary tells him. At that the minister closes the file. "I'm not exactly sure what all you're doing in our country," he says, "but whatever it is, just carry on." And so he does, for more than eighteen years.

Another missionary attends a summit meeting of five major southeast Asian nations held in the Muslim nation of more than fifty million people where he ministers. Muslim, Buddhist, Hindu, and Christian leaders are asked to pray and read their scriptures. After the missionary prays positively and passionately for the country in front of its leaders, all periodic government investigation into his background ceases, and he is no longer required to submit his radio manuscripts for scrutiny. He now has carte blanche. For the last twenty-nine years he has freely preached the gospel there. In fact, Muslim government officials send their children to his day school. His church, which began with four widows, is now the largest in the country. We believe this is all because he followed the scriptural injunction to pray positively for government:

> Here are my directions: Pray much for others; plead for God's mercy upon them; give thanks for all he is going to do for them. *Pray in this way* for kings and all others who are in authority over us, or are in places of high responsibility, so that we can live in peace and quietness, spending our time in godly living and thinking much about the Lord.
>
> 1 Timothy 2:1–2 TLB, emphasis added

102

J. B. Phillips translates the next two verses of this passage like this:

> In the sight of God our Savior this is undoubtedly the right thing to pray for; for *his purpose is that all men should be saved and come to realize the truth.*
>
> 1 Timothy 2:3–4 PHILLIPS, emphasis added

Derek Prince, in his powerful book *Shaping History through Prayer and Fasting,* outlines this same Scripture in a series of simple, logical steps and tells why they are so important:

1. The first ministry and outreach of believers meeting together in regular fellowship is prayer.
2. The first specific topic for prayer is government.
3. We are to pray for good government.
4. God wants all men to have the gospel preached to them.
5. Good government facilitates the preaching of the gospel while bad government hinders it.
6. Therefore good government is the will of God.[19]

Good government gives us freedom of speech and assembly, maintains law and order, and allows unrestricted communication and travel. All these are vital to the propagation of the gospel. So God tells us to pray earnestly for good government so that people might be saved.

Satan, on the other hand, wants to keep people from hearing or responding to the gospel. Therefore he uses lawmakers to restrict the influence of Christianity and the Bible, while "liberating" society into depravity through permissive legislation toward obscenity, pornography, public immorality, and demonic religions and through leniency toward criminal acts. These ultimately lead to the breakdown of moral and ethical restrictions. The sex for sale and crime on our streets, the corruption in our government, the godlessness in our classrooms, and the titillating filth in films and television touch us all. When we are exposed to a society in which depravity is accepted so casually, we gradually become hardened to it: "Beware then of your own hearts, dear brothers, lest you find that they, too, are evil and unbelieving and are leading you away from the living God. Speak to each other . . . every day while there is still time, so that none of you will become hardened against God, being blinded by the glamor of sin" (Heb. 3:12–13 TLB).

Like Lot who, living in Sodom, "vexed his righteous soul from day to day with their unlawful deeds" (2 Peter 2:8 KJV), shouldn't we be vexed to the heart by the vileness in our society? If Christians, particularly intercessors, become hardened and rebellious, Satan has won and our society is lost.

Intercessors are the lifeline of the church and the nation as they "pray much" for those in authority, "plead for God's mercy" on them, and "give thanks for all he is going to do for them." These are prayers from the heart of God, who wants everyone to come to repentance and to the knowledge of the truth.

Not only do we need to pray for those in authority, we need to let them know we are out there and we are paying attention to what they do. They don't need hate letters and ugliness from us; they need strong but sensible and civil opinions. They need encouragement and correction from concerned and supportive citizens.

The church has the ability and responsibility to speak out and then to pray that our legislators will stop legalizing sin, or to ask God for new lawmakers who will, before our national unrighteousness becomes the death of us.

The Ball Is in Our Court

We know that there is no government anywhere that God has not put in power (Rom. 13:1), either to bless or to chastise, and that God rules over the kingdoms of this world and gives them to whomever he chooses to rule (Dan. 4:17). We also know that if we ask for anything in God's will, we can be sure he will answer us (1 John 5:14). Finally, we know that good government is his will because it serves the propagation of the gospel. This means that God is willing to move on behalf of the nation. He always moves in cooperation with his praying people; that puts the ball directly in our court.

Government, however, isn't the only arena of influence that heavily influences our lives and demands our intercession. Loren Cunningham, founder of Youth with a Mission (YWAM), has identified what he calls the seven mind-molders of society:

- Family
- Government
- Media
- Education
- Business
- Religion
- Arts and entertainment

The battle for the soul of a nation rages in all of these institutions. Intercession and involvement—or apathy— will determine which kingdom rules in our society.

Prayer priority 1: Pray for all those in positions of influence who are standing for righteousness, especially legislators whom you know to be Christians. They need dedicated prayer support and strong fellowship to avoid the pitfalls of political power. It is easy to become more interested in reelection than in righteousness.

Prayer priority 2: Pray for those who champion ungodly causes, that they will change their ways or be removed from their places of influence. Satan works in those who are disobedient to God (see Eph. 2:2). Anyone who doesn't obey the gospel is a potential pawn in the battle for the nation.

Prayer priority 3: Pray about the possibility of personal involvement in influential arenas, including the political process. It is vital for Christians in a democracy not only to pray for those in authority but to pray for many educated, prepared, and righteous persons to *become* those in authority. When we elect the ungodly to positions of power, we lose by default the right to make and interpret the laws under which we and our children have to live.

Since we know about the importance of confessing the failures of the nation, why not begin that right now? Here is our prayer on behalf of the above seven institutions in our own country, the United States. (If you are from another country, you may adapt it to suit the situation there.) You may want to list the points of confession from this prayer and amplify a few of them at different prayer sessions instead of covering the whole list at once. You may also want to read the prayer aloud if you're working with a Bible study/prayer group or partner. It covers many issues, so focus your mind and spirit for a season of intercession. We encourage you to pray with faith and excitement about what God is going to do through you.

Prayer of Intercession for the Nation

Father, on behalf of our nation, we confess that we have offended you disgracefully with our ungodliness. We have become thankless, rebellious, and unclean. We have ignored your guidance and spurned your presence. We have become a hedonistic, violent, greedy people. Our foolishness has led us to the brink of destruction. O God, forgive us and deliver us! We pray earnestly, desperately, and expectantly for a massive spiritual awakening and transformation in America.

Father, bless and move upon all the leaders of our nation. Stir and transform their minds and make them righteous and wise. Pull down from power those with inflexible hearts who set their faces against you. Replace them with those who will be led by your Spirit and your principles. Give these new leaders wisdom, grace, and courage. Protect them and their families from every ungodly influence and attack. Bless and prosper them and bring their righteous plans to fruition.

Establish truth in our educational systems and give us godly teachers and educators who will be righteous role models for our children. Remove those who bring immorality, heresy, or occultism into our classrooms.

Give us integrity, fairness, and truth in our news media.

We ask for righteous judgment in our courts, with equal justice for everyone in our society. Particularly in our Supreme Court, bring your influence to bear. Give these judges revelation, wisdom, and courage to make godly and righteous decisions. Give us righteous attorneys who desire justice and truth more than personal gain.

Move sovereignly in the media and arts and entertainment industries. Pull down the ungodly and raise up men and women of your choice in this arena of unprecedented influence. Redeem it for your own; let it encourage righteousness and be a tool for spiritual ingathering.

Heal our homes and cement our family relationships. Help us to "do love" there, above all. Fill our homes with wisdom, fairness, compassion, affection, and fun.

Deliver the children who are subjected to abuse and fear and who are led into sin by those who should be their defenders. Protect them with your angels, Father, and heal their wounded hearts.

Help us with wisdom, power, and love to take back the liberties the church has lost to those who neither know nor respect you.

Protect and encourage the Christian heroes of our nation, those who face threats and persecution as they confront the viciousness of entrenched depravity in their given arenas of influence.

Heal the soul of America. May it once again truly be "one nation under God," filled with your glory. Amen.

Thinking It Over

1. How do you feel about the scriptural principle that God controls governments? What does that tell you about your responsibility and involvement as a Christian?

2. On what basis does God deal with nations?

3. Is Daniel's practice of identifying with the sins of the nation a valid one for the church?

4. Do most of the Christians you know make it a regular practice to pray for the nation and the government? If not, why not?

5. If God has given the church a mandate to pray for good government, what can the average Christian do to help the church understand and assume that responsibility?

6. Could you explain to someone else the connection between good government and evangelism?

Suggestions for Prayer

- Pray the intercession prayer for the nation at the end of this chapter.
- Pray for the three prayer priorities listed in this chapter.
- Pray for the seven mind-molders listed in this chapter.

10

Fasting: Supercharged Prayer

Imagine the dramatic and traumatic experience of the prophet Jonah: Vomited from the sea, he appears in Nineveh shaken, angry, bleached white from his time in the belly of a fish, and smelling terrible. He is a wild apparition. His message is terrifying, if you believe him; no wasted words, no offer of hope, simply, "Forty more days and Nineveh will be overturned" (Jonah 3:4 NIV).

Lo and behold, the Ninevites believe him! They declare a fast and all of them, from the greatest to the least, put on sackcloth. Their heathen king sits down in the dust and issues a proclamation: "Nobody eat or drink anything. Turn from your evil and call urgently on God for mercy" (see vv. 7–9). God does hear them and mercifully rescinds his sentence of destruction.

Angry Prophets and Fasting Kings

Jonah, who hates the Ninevites, is so furious that he wants to die. "I *knew* you'd do that; that's why I didn't want to come!" he rails at God. "I knew you were a gracious God, merciful, slow to get angry, and full of kindness. I knew how easily you could cancel your plans for destroying these people!" (see Jonah 4:1–2).

God rebukes Jonah's anger: "Nineveh has more than a hundred and twenty thousand people who cannot tell their right hand from their left. . . . Should I not be concerned about that great city?" (Jonah 4:11 NIV).

It would be hard to find a better example of the efficacy of fasting. As a powerful measure for answered prayer, nothing beats it. Used according to God's conditions, fasting has seldom failed to bring about restoration, deliverance, and victory. For instance, when word comes to King Jehoshaphat that three enemy nations have formed a coalition army against Judah and are only days away, he is terrified. But he does the right thing: He seeks the Lord. Then he holds a nationwide prayer meeting and proclaims a fast throughout the kingdom, including men, women, and children.

God's response is swift: "Don't be afraid, the battle isn't yours but God's. March down against them. . . . You won't have to fight. . . . Stand still and watch God deliver you." When they arrive at the war zone, they find that God has turned the invaders against one another, and instead of facing a sea of glittering spears, they find only a vast army of corpses. Judah spends three days gathering up the spoils and then lives on in peace for years afterward (see 2 Chron. 20:1–24).

Fasting was a familiar practice to all the Old Testament Jews. Through years of experience they learned the effectiveness of fasting and prayer in times of both

111

personal and national crisis. They fasted and prayed for many reasons:

- Restoration of the nation (see Neh. 1:4)
- Deliverance from their enemies (see 2 Chron. 20:3; Esther 4:16)
- Deliverance from God's judgment (see Jonah 3:5; Joel 2:12)

Follow the Leader

The sun refracts the water into a million prisms as Jesus stands in the Jordan, praying, and a divine dove glides downward through the glory of the opened heavens. As the Holy Spirit settles upon him, the audible, awesome voice of God declares, "You are My Son, My Beloved! In You I am well pleased and find delight!" (Luke 3:22 AB).

Surely this breathtaking empowering at Jesus' baptism should launch him straight into his miraculous ministry. But it does not. First comes the fast—forty days and forty nights. Only then, when he has overcome his own appetites, is he ready to overcome the challenges of Satan and face his own destiny (see Luke 4:1–2).

In the Sermon on the Mount (see Matthew 5–7), Jesus takes for granted that his followers will fast, even as he takes for granted that they will pray and give to the needy:

- *When* you give . . . (see 6:3)
- *When* you pray . . . (see 6:5)
- *When* you fast . . . (see 6:17)

Notice he says when, not if. These are directives, not suggestions.

112

The apostle Paul, determinedly disciplining his body, fasted often, knowing he could not have victory over the enemy until he had victory over his flesh (see 1 Cor. 9:27). The early church fasted to lend weight to their worship and to receive revelation and direction from God (see Acts 13:1–3). If all these leaders needed it, surely we do, too.

We've all experienced times when our praying seems to hit an impasse and our words bounce off the ceiling, or extreme situations in which prayer alone doesn't seem to be getting the job done. It is for these times that God has given us fasting—both private and united public fasting—with prayer.

Unfortunately, this practice has been all but lost to large segments of the church. Because it has been associated with legalism and asceticism on one hand and with meaningless ritualism on the other, "thinking" Christians have thrown the baby out with the bathwater by disassociating themselves from the practice of fasting altogether.

But today the Holy Spirit is calling the church to fast. We see it happening all over the country. Considering both the crisis times in which we live and the possibility of imminent and perhaps unprecedented revival, every intercessor needs a balanced biblical perspective of this powerful exercise, and the know-how to use it under the Holy Spirit's guidance, both to thwart the plans of the devil and to undergird the moving of God.

How Do We Do It?

For our fasting to be effective, we need to do more than just abstain from eating. At the risk of being repetitive, we must remind you that the fast—or self-denial— that impresses God includes life intercession:

113

- Freeing the oppressed
- Feeding the hungry
- Housing the homeless
- Clothing the naked
- Speaking the truth
- Walking in humility
- Providing for our families
- Refraining from gossip
- Being just, fair, and righteous

In return for our obedience, God has promised us revelation, healing, guidance, protection, provision, and promptly answered prayer. A generous return on our investment, wouldn't you say? If we're not receiving these blessings and can't understand why, it might be wise to go back and use Isaiah 58, "God's chosen fast," as a personal checklist. It may provide some clues.

What exactly do we mean when we refer to fasting? Let's look at some definitions of the word and then move on to some practical suggestions for effective fasting. The dictionary definition for *fast* is: "To abstain from food; to eat sparingly or to abstain from some foods." Here are three biblical types of fasts:

- *The total fast:* abstaining from all food and water (see Deut. 9:9, 18; Ezra 10:6; Esther 4:16; Acts 9:9)
- *The normal fast:* abstaining from food but not from water (see 1 Kings 19:8; 2 Chron. 20:3; Matt. 4:2)
- *The partial fast:* eating sparingly or abstaining from some foods (see Dan. 10:2–3)

Know that however you choose to begin fasting, it won't be easy. The following tips will help you prepare and persevere.

Be prepared for a struggle. Take, for example, the preacher who had been on a long fast and was having a battle with a serious appetite. Staunchly he persevered. As he got up to speak at a meeting on the last day of his fast, his stomach had finally had it and put up a loud and ongoing protest during his message. The audience thought it was hilarious but the preacher did not. As soon as he got off the platform, he and his stomach had a showdown. "All right, you," he snarled, glaring down at the vicinity of his navel. "That kind of behavior will get you nowhere. Just to teach you a lesson, we're going to fast an extra day!" And they did.

Begin with short fasts, perhaps only a meal or two, and graduate to longer ones. Try partial fasts, such as Daniel's, at first.

Don't go without liquids for more than three days. This seems to be the biblical limit. Longer abstinence may seriously harm your body. Moses abstained from water for two periods of forty days each, but he was supernaturally sustained by God while in his immediate presence.

Don't fast at all without consulting your physician if you have serious physical problems such as diabetes.

Break your fast carefully. Eat lightly at first. If you've been on a long fast, begin by taking only liquids. Then take a few days to get back to normal eating patterns. This is a good time to break the habit of overeating.

You may be like the food-loving fellow who gets a headache and feels faint if he misses lunch. But it's no joke when the body begins to react to some real food deprivation. People who use a lot of sugar or caffeine often have the most difficulty. It's a good idea to cut down gradually on these for a few days before you actually begin to fast.

Remember, the extremely long, complete fasts achieved by Moses, Elijah, and Jesus were undertaken only by special revelation and supernatural empowerment from the Lord. Don't try this unless you too have a special revelation from God. All fasting should be led of the Spirit. Be careful not to let it become ritualized or legalistic. If you're fasting to receive guidance, it's wise not to act on any decisions until you have broken the fast, especially if it's a long one. You will then be able to evaluate more clearly what the Lord has shown you.

When you fast, pray for the hungry. Once you've experienced a little of how they feel, you'll be able to intercede more effectively for them. And how about interceding with the money you would have spent for food by giving it to Christian relief organizations who will use it to feed those who are starving? You'll be fulfilling part of God's chosen fast.

Victory in this battle with our appetites stands us in good stead as we push on toward victory in the battle with Satan.

Thinking It Over

1. After reading this chapter, do you think fasting is a valid, spiritually powerful practice for the church today?

2. If fasting hasn't been a practice with you, are you willing to try it in some form?

3. How do you think fasting might strengthen you spiritually?

4. Would you like to see corporate prayer and fasting practiced by your own church for vital spiritual and national issues?

5. Would you be willing to urge your church to initiate or become involved with corporate prayer and fasting on behalf of the nation?

6. What have been your experiences with prayer and fasting? What were the results?

7. Do a personal checkup using God's chosen fast: freeing the oppressed; housing the homeless; speaking the truth; providing for our families; feeding the hungry; clothing the naked; walking in humility; refraining from gossip; being just, fair, and righteous. How did you do?

Suggestions for Prayer

- Ask God for wisdom and the willingness to use fasting as a power tool in prayer, both for yourself and for your church.
- Pray for local school board members.
- Pray for the national news media.

PART 3

Fighting the Fight

The monks have no sadness. They wage war on the devil as though they were performing a dance.

John Chrysostom

11

Spiritual Warfare: Recognizing the Enemy

Home from the army with a Section Eight discharge, the personable kid who enlisted two years earlier has "morphed" into a mumbling, wary-eyed stranger. Before long he begins stalking one of the young women in his church. His distraught parents take him to physicians and psychiatrists, but to no avail. After months of struggle, the boy's father comes to my husband and asks what he would do if the boy were his son. Frankly, Jimmy says, he would get him to a pastor who understands demonic deliverance. The father hasn't wanted to face that possibility, but in his heart he too believes that is the answer.

Then the family's pastor hears what Jimmy has suggested. He is furious. He calls the family in and declares that there are no such things as demons—despite the fact that his denomination has produced wonderful material on spiritual warfare. He denounces Jimmy's advice as superstitious nonsense and tells the family to forget it. They obey their pastor.

Months later, muttering to himself, eyes shaking like grapes in a bowl of Jell-O, the young man is institutionalized. There he remains for years with no sign of improvement, finally committing suicide.

Facing Spiritual Facts

Of course, most mental illness has physical or psychological roots, and try as you will, you can't cast out a chemical imbalance. Usually we need to examine other possibilities carefully before we decide there is a demonic source. But when we are unable or unwilling to recognize problems rooted in demonic oppression, spiritual warfare is never waged and those problems are never solved. When we consider ourselves too sophisticated to believe in a real devil, we become easy prey.

The prophets, the apostles, and Jesus himself say that Satan is a real, live spiritual being. Once we accept that, we must understand what he is *not*. Satan is not a kind of Darth Vader of the spiritual world, the dark counterpart of the Force: all-knowing, all-powerful, ever present evil. He is a created being with limited powers who can be in only one place at a time. Only rarely will he personally bother with most of us. Unless we are doing major damage to his kingdom, we will probably be relegated to the attentions of lesser spiritual powers. In this book, however, we may use the terms Satan or the devil in the generic sense of referring to any or all of his subordinates.

To illustrate: C. Peter Wagner, in *Warfare Prayer*, pictures an American soldier in the Persian Gulf shouting, "Here we come, Sadam Hussein!" Wagner explains, "None of the soldiers ever expected to see Sadam Hussein personally, but they did declare who the real enemy was. . . . Jesus cast a spirit of infirmity out of a woman. Explaining what He had done, He said that Satan had kept her bound 18 years. I don't think He meant that Satan himself had spent 18 years demonizing that woman, but as commander-in-chief of the forces of evil, he had ultimately been responsible for delegating that task to a spirit of infirmity."[20]

Once we recognize the presence and work of this very real enemy, we can deal with him firmly and effectively and see tangible results, as Jimmy and I can testify.

We had just bought a house at a bargain price. The former owners gave new meaning to the term "dysfunctional family": The rebellious, always-in-trouble teenagers had seriously trashed the place, their father had gone bankrupt and needed open-heart surgery, and finally, their mother had died there. The father and the kids were moving to Florida to start over.

We loved the house from the start, but the atmosphere was heavy, oppressive, and uneasy. When we found occult books that had been left behind, we called in the troops—our church elders—to help us give the place a spiritual housecleaning. This was our method:

- We claimed the benefits of the blood of Jesus over us.
- We put on our spiritual armor (see Eph. 6:10–20).
- We went through all the rooms, telling the enemy, in Jesus' name, that the kingdom of God was moving in and he must move out.
- We invited the Holy Spirit to take up residence wherever any demonic powers had made their habitation.
- We took time in each room to give high praise to God.

A few days later two of our new neighbor ladies, one Jewish and one Catholic, dropped in for a get-acquainted visit. After some polite preliminary remarks, one of them burst out with, "What have you done in here?"

"What do you mean?" we asked.

"Well," said the other woman, "we don't mean to say anything out of line, but this place used to be . . . I don't know . . . creepy!"

"You did something, didn't you?" the first lady persisted. We told them about our "housecleaning" method with the church elders. It all made perfect sense to them. They could feel the difference and they accepted it without question.

Then we had a visit from the oldest daughter of the previous owner, who had stayed in town to finish her senior year in high school. One sunny morning she knocked on the front door.

"I'm getting ready to go to Florida," she explained, "and I wonder if I could come in for one last look at the house before I go."

"Of course," we said. "Come on in."

The girl walked into the entry hall, chatting about her plans, then suddenly stopped dead in her tracks. Her eyes and her mouth flew wide open.

"You did it," she whispered.

"What? What did we do?"

"You did it," she repeated. "I can't believe it! You broke the jinx in this house, didn't you?"

She was dumbfounded that the demonic powers that had "jinxed" her family were bound and gone, and we were amazed that she had so instantly sensed their absence. Although she wasn't a Christian, she readily acknowledged that the power of Jesus Christ had dramatically changed things in that house.

However, Satan's scope goes far beyond vulnerable young soldiers, dysfunctional families, and demon-infested houses. His influence is global and the battle is cosmic.

A Cosmic Confrontation

Like something straight out of a Frank Peretti novel, the angel Gabriel wages a titanic struggle to reach the prophet Daniel with an answer to prayer. You can almost hear the shriek of steel and see the flares of cosmic light as the mighty angel of God struggles with the "Prince of Persia," the powerful, malevolent spirit who overrules that kingdom. For three weeks the angel fights, but he can't break through. Then Michael, the "Prince of Israel," one of God's chief angelic warrior princes, streaks out of heaven to join Gabriel in the battle. Together they smash through the spiritual blockade. Moreover, after delivering his message to Daniel, Gabriel prepares to battle his way back again, past both the Prince of Persia and the Prince of Greece, where the angel prince, Michael, again joins him in the warfare (see Dan. 10:11–13).

The apostle Paul says that our enemies, like Daniel's, are not "flesh and blood, but . . . persons without bodies—the evil rulers of the unseen world, those mighty satanic beings and great evil princes of darkness who rule this world . . . huge numbers of wicked spirits in the spirit world" (Eph. 6:12 TLB). That's *The Living Bible's* version. Other translations refer to them as "world rulers," "despotisms," "cosmic powers," "potentates of the dark world," and "organizations and powers that are spiritual."

These titles reaffirm what Daniel learned—that Satan's kingdom is organized. So is God's angelic kingdom. Therefore within each of these kingdoms there is a powerful and dedicated support system for the warfare. (The church seems to be the one spiritual force that hasn't quite got the unity and cooperation principle sorted out.)

Ephesians 6:12 says that we also wrestle with spiritual principalities, or with the chief ruling spirits over those principalities. A physical principality is a territory such as Monaco, ruled over by a prince. It is the same in the spirit realm. Isn't it reasonable to suppose that today, as in Daniel's time, nations have assigned to them satanic princes whose purpose it is to control its people and affairs?

One of Jimmy's most vivid experiences of this kind of spiritual warfare took place on the west steps of the United States Capitol. He was conducting one of our musicals with a huge choir at a Flag Day celebration. At the beginning of the spiritual warfare section, he was caught up in the message of the lyrics:

Keep looking down, we're seated in the heavenlies;
God's mighty power has raised us over all!
Keep looking down, above all principalities,
For we have died and risen with the Lord!
And in his name we have authority
And in his name we shall prevail.
And in his name we dare to face the enemy
And in his name we cannot fail!

Next, lots of spiritual warfare Scriptures were read over the pulsating music and then—*Bang!*—straight into the next song:

You are the children of the kingdom of God,
You're the chosen ones for whom the Savior came.
You're his noble new creation by the Spirit and the
  blood,
You're the church that he has built to bear his name!
And the gates of hell shall not prevail against you!
And the hordes of darkness cannot quench your light!
And the hosts of God shall stand and fight beside you
Till your king shall reign triumphant in his might!

126

Jimmy explains, "As I conducted, I was feeling the strength and truth of the songs and gazing upward with a tremendous rush of love at the great Capitol dome, with its flags flying against the sky. That dome is the symbol of the seat of government of the country I love. Then like a bolt the awareness hit me: It also represents the seat of the Prince of America, the very front lines of the battle for the soul of my nation. Here he and a hierarchy of evil persons without bodies are working tirelessly to control the minds of countless government officials, staff workers, lobbyists, strategists, advisors, and other people of influence. There are probably more demons and angels doing their work in that building than anywhere else in the country.

"Suddenly I was directing, praying, and warring in the spirit all at the same time. What was happening in my spirit somehow connected with the choir. You could hear it in their voices and see it on their faces, and they rose to magnificent heights. It was a hair-standing-on-end moment of spiritual power, written in my heart forever. When I pray for our government, I often look back on it with awe."

National Confrontation

Imagine an Asian coastline with an island some distance offshore. Straddling the two is a powerful giant with bronzed, muscular arms crossed on a massive chest—a kind of cosmic Mr. Clean. He has a beautiful but arrogant Asian face, hard as stone. This is the visual impression I had as I prayed at home one day for China.

"Who is this?" I asked the Lord.

The answer came clearly to my mind: "This is the covering spirit that stands over against the gateway to the East."

It seemed clear that here is an ancient spiritual ruler, well entrenched and completely confident of his authority.

"Shall I pray against him?" I asked.

The answer was hasty: "No, no, no! This one is for the church to pray against. Tell the pastor."

I told our pastor, Jack Hayford, and the church began to pray unitedly for this dominating spirit over China to be deposed and for Jesus Christ to be enthroned in his rightful place as Lord.

We believe revelation regarding the spiritual bondage of China was given to many churches and prayer groups at that time, and only after persistent corporate intercession and warfare have we seen China once again opening to the gospel.

This "spiritually political" kind of praying involves fighting against very powerful spiritual beings and should usually be a corporate undertaking. Under the leadership of the Holy Spirit, we must learn when to tackle something alone and when to pray corporately. Then we won't be presumptuous and get in over our heads in spiritual warfare. United fasting and prayer and a thorough understanding of our ruling position in Christ are crucial.

We should note here that while Satan and other great spiritual authorities are never to be feared by those who belong to Christ and walk in obedience to God, neither should they be taken lightly. Nor, in the protocol of the spiritual kingdoms, should they be insulted or reviled by any of us (see 2 Peter 2:10–11; Jude 8–10). Deal with them as ambassadors of God's kingdom should, contending with boldness, unflinching determination, and absolute authority, but never with scorn or ridicule.

But don't be intimidated. We have certainly been authorized to fight this fight, and we don't need to be afraid to do it. We can pray confidently and with authority against all the works of the devil. The most effective thing we can do to dislodge him and destroy his strongholds is to glorify, honor, and magnify God, acknowledging his supremacy over all other powers and invoking and inviting his divine presence. When God really shows up, all other powers release their prisoners and flee. "Where the Spirit of the Lord is, there is liberty" (2 Cor. 3:17 KJV).

Thinking It Over

1. Has reading this chapter changed your thinking in any way about Satan and his activities? How?
2. What do you think of our experience in spiritually cleansing our house? Can you see the effectiveness of our method? Have you ever used similar methods? How did they work?
3. Do you feel there is validity to the idea of a hierarchy of spiritual beings involving themselves with human governments? Are there specific instances in which you feel there might be satanic authority at work in our government?
4. How do you see satanic influence working in our society's seven mind-molders listed in chapter 9?

Suggestions for Prayer

- Ask for wisdom and courage as you take on the warfare challenge.
- Ask for cleansing as you confess any known sin and prepare your heart for intercession.
- Pray for the educational system: teachers, administrators, curricula writers and publishers, and so on.
- Pray for other mind molders.

12

Taking Charge

To whom God would make known what is the riches of the glory of this mystery among the Gentiles; which is *Christ in you, the hope of glory.*

Colossians 1:27 KJV, emphasis added

Well, You know I'm not a fighter, Lord,
And the hosts of hell are strong.
So fill me with your Spirit,
Help me put my armor on.
And when I face the enemy,
All that he will see
Is me standin' there in you
And you standin' there in me.

"The Victor"
Jimmy and Carol Owens

Mark Twain's classic *The Prince and the Pauper* is the story of a royal mix-up, a case of mistaken identity. A beggar, the spitting image of a young prince who has run away, is mistakenly taken from the streets, scrubbed and groomed, and put on the throne. He is scared stiff. Surely they can see I'm nobody, he thinks. Surely I'll be discovered and executed. He soon realizes, however, that because everybody identifies him with the real prince, all the prince's authority is at his disposal. He is now the man with the power.

Mistaken Identity

Like the pauper, our authority is not in ourselves but in our identification with our Prince. In the eyes of both God and Satan, we are one with Christ. The church fathers experienced that "identification authority" and used it to change the world. Having known its reality and dynamism, they share it with us:

> We were *dead and buried with him* in baptism, so that just as he was raised from the dead by that splendid revelation of the Father's power so *we too might rise* to life on a new plane altogether. . . . Let us never forget that our old selves *died with him* on the cross that the tyranny of sin over us might be broken—for a dead man can safely be said to be immune to the power of sin.

> Romans 6:4–8 PHILLIPS, emphasis added

> And He raised us up *together with Him* and made us sit down *together* giving us joint seating with Him in the heavenly sphere by virtue of our being in Christ Jesus (the Messiah, the Anointed One).

> Ephesians 2:6 AB, emphasis added

In the reality of the spiritual world, the head (Christ) and his body (the church) are crucified, resurrected, ascended, and enthroned together in the place of highest spiritual authority. This should always be our point of view: *above* every power and principality that is named.

If we don't stand in that position, Satan will come along and eat our lunch regularly. But once we put our identification authority to work by faith, we begin to "reign in life through . . . Jesus Christ" (Rom. 5:17 NIV). Then our lives are changed forever. Satan's will be changed, too, as he is progressively challenged and dethroned.

If you declare this truth right out loud every day of your life, it will cause your faith to soar and it will demoralize the enemy. You can declare, *It is written: I am dead indeed to sin, but alive to God in Jesus Christ my Lord* (see Rom. 6:11) or *It is written: I have been crucified with Christ; it is no longer I who live, but Christ lives in me* (see Gal. 2:20).

When we claim our death to sin and stand in Christ, claiming his purity and power as our own, we are ready to go to war under God's flag. We are then "fair as the moon, clear as the sun, and terrible as an army with banners" (Song of Sol. 6:10 KJV).[21]

Intercession: The Call to War

Most of us are peace-loving souls who prefer God's green pastures and still waters to armies and banners and battlefields. You may even want to take exception to Paul, who refers to Christians as soldiers (see 2 Tim. 2:3). Certainly, few of us are the prepared, dedicated soldiers God is longing for, ready to give everything and take whatever comes. We'd like to skip the parts about taking our share of suffering. We'd prefer not to hear God say, "Do not let yourself become tied up in worldly affairs, for then you cannot satisfy the one who has enlisted you in his army" (2 Tim. 2:4 TLB).

Real dedication calls for major changes in focus and attitude. Satan is "the god of this world" (see 2 Cor. 4:4)

and the "ruler of the darkness of this world" (see Eph.
6:12). He controls how the world thinks and behaves. If
we are living by the world's mind-set and values, we will
be too vulnerable to the enemy to be useful to God.
Unfortunately, while we live on this planet there's no
place to hide from the bombardment of the world; it's
just part of the war. There is, however, another secret of
spiritual victory to go along with our identification with
Christ and our declaration that in him we are dead to
sin and alive to God: "Submit yourselves therefore to
God. Resist the devil, and he will flee from you" (James
4:7 kjv).

Give God control of everything you have and are.
Then resist the devil in Jesus' name, right out loud if
necessary. (Martin Luther once heaved an inkwell at
him, but we don't recommend that method.) Just tell
him who you are, whom you serve, and who your God
is: the creative, sustaining, ruling force of the universe,
who is the final authority in heaven and earth. And you
are his representative. Say so!

Sometimes resisting the devil is not a matter of struggle and debate but simply of nonresponse to those first
whispers of temptation, avoiding trouble before it starts.
Ogden Nash, a poet with a shrewd but cockeyed view of
human nature, put it succinctly:

> When called by a panther,
> . . . Don't anther.

Dethroning the Devil

The greatest agency [God has] put in man's hands is
prayer. And to define prayer, one must use the language
of war. Peace language is not equal to the situation. *The
earth is in a state of war and is being hotly besieged.* Thus
one must use war talk to grasp the facts with which

prayer is concerned. Prayer from God's side is communication between Himself and His allies in enemy country.

S. D. Gordon, emphasis added

What is spiritual warfare really all about? The objective is not to fight demons but to save souls—souls under siege. These are the spoils we wrest from the enemy and carry home to the King. World evangelization is the cry of God's heart, and it remains the great unfinished calling of the church. It is within our power to fulfill the Great Commission in our generation. The technology is there if only we will use it; the money is there if only we will give it; the manpower is there if only we will go.

However, the goal will not be reached without intense and persevering struggle. Propagating the gospel is a declaration of war against Satan and his works, and it engenders bitter spiritual opposition. So we must undertake the work of restraining the forces of darkness until God's purposes of redemption are complete. This is a spiritual struggle and it is the job of the intercessor:

> That day [the Day of the Lord] cannot come before the final rebellion against God, when wickedness will be revealed in human form, the man doomed to perdition. *He is the Enemy . . . you must now be aware of the restraining hand which ensures that he shall be revealed only at the proper time.* For already the secret power of wickedness is at work, secret only for the present until the Restrainer disappears from the scene. And then he will be revealed, that wicked man whom the Lord Jesus will destroy with the breath of his mouth, and annihilate by the radiance of his coming.

2 Thessalonians 2:3–4, 6–9 NEB, emphasis added

The Holy Spirit, working through the church, is the restraining hand that prevents immediate world domination by Satan through his political puppet, the Antichrist. As long as we live in this world, we need to be about our part in this ongoing work, a potent prayer force that is a devastating threat to Satan's plans of world domination. As Peter Beyerhaus writes, "Any advancement of the kingdom of Christ takes place by successive dethronement of Satan."[22]

When we speak of dethroning Satan, we don't mean his final defeat at the return of Jesus. We're talking about the dethronement that comes as we progressively take back enemy territory and wreak havoc in his camp. One preacher says that his greatest ambition is to make so much serious trouble for Satan's kingdom that when his eyes open every morning, the demons will scream, "Red alert! Red alert! He's awaaaake!" Harold Lindsell writes,

> Although Satan's work is not yet finished and his doom [is] still in the future, God has put a leash on him. He can go only so far and no further.
>
> There is the mystery of why God permits Satan to continue for as much as another hour, or why he fits into the cosmic plan of salvation. Nevertheless, God assures His people that He is for them and greater than the one who is against them, that Satan's doom is sure, that he is to be resisted by the people of God (James 4:7), and that for them there is victory over the wicked one.[23]

God has put this restraining leash in the hands of the church. It is up to us to use it.

13

Restraining the Enemy

"Come back here, you little wart!" I yelled as I chased Bobby down the street. Bobby was a five-year-old wild man who had decided to streak the neighborhood and was careening across lawns and through hedges, shedding his clothes along the way. I was his harassed teenage baby-sitter. After finally getting him treed and carrying him bodily back to the house, I attempted to get him dressed again. Not a chance. Slick as an eel, he wormed away and dashed for the toy box where he armed himself with a baseball bat. Although he looked like an angel, he had a killer's heart, and the chase quickly turned in the other direction. I headed rapidly for the kitchen, where I distracted him with something chocolate, then disarmed him.

When his parents returned, I told them I was breaking off our business relationship. But out of pity for them (and as a practical joke on my friend) I gave them Shirley's name as a replacement.

Sure enough, they called Shirley; Shirley called me. "Hi," she said, "I'm over at the Smiths', baby-sitting Bobby."

"Lucky you," I said. "How's it going?"

There seemed to be some muffled shouting in the background, but Shirley sounded cheerful enough. "No problem," she replied.

"No problem?" I asked. "What did you do, burn his baseball bat?"

"Well, I tried to coax it away from him," she explained, "but nothing worked. So after I let him chase me around in here for a while, I got an old jump rope out of the toy box, tackled him, and tied him to his little rocking chair. He's in there rocking and hollering like mad. And that's where he's gonna stay till Mommy gets home."

Using the Leash

Now, although I wouldn't recommend this method of child care, the kicker to the story is that Shirley became Bobby's permanent baby-sitter. You see, unlike my teenage self, Shirley was a great little restrainer who didn't fool around; she simply bound up the opposition. When it comes to dealing with Satan, that should be our method, too. Jesus said we can't rob a strong man's house without first binding up the strong man (see Matt. 12:29; Mark 3:27).

The inevitable question is, How in the world do we do it? "Whatever you bind (declare to be improper and unlawful) on earth must be what is *already bound* in heaven; and whatever you loose (declare lawful) on earth must be what is *already loosed* in heaven" (Matt. 16:19 AB, emphasis added).

How do we know what has already been bound and loosed in heaven? Well, we have some strong scriptural clues. At Jesus' ascension *"He led captivity captive*—He led a train of vanquished foes—and He bestowed gifts on men"* (Eph. 4:8 AB, emphasis added). Matthew Henry's commentary on this verse is, "He conquered those who had conquered us."

On the cross, Jesus discarded the spiritual potentates and powers like so many old clothes and made a public display of them by leading them as captives (in other words, bound up) in his triumphal procession (see Col. 2:15). What a cosmic upheaval!

Then, to add insult to Satan's injury, Jesus shares with all us weak, fallible mortals the benefits of his victory over the kingdom of darkness by giving us the authority to bind them on earth as they have already been bound in heaven.

The church is actually an occupation army, an alien, ruling agency within a nation, enforcing the will of our absent King and restraining the opposition. We do this through intercessory warfare prayer. We bind them by *declaration* made by faith in Jesus' victory.

Part of Jesus' messianic call was to release the prisoners—those who are bound—from the dungeon (see Isa. 42:7). We loose the prisoners of sin through the gospel. Where there is enemy oppression in any situation, we can invoke the presence of the Lord and loose his liberating authority, for where the Spirit of the Lord is, there is freedom.

Our Legal Authority

Here are some simple spiritual legalities:

- Satan's "cease and desist" warrant has been signed by Jesus Christ, but he has appointed the church to serve it.

- The court of heaven has approved the eviction no-tice, but the church has been appointed to deliver and enforce it.
- The legalities of divine jurisdiction have been taken care of by the resurrected Lord, but he has appointed the church to put them into action.

In giving us such authority, God is teaching us how to reign with him and is preparing us for an eternal future of rulership.

We bind the enemy by using the command of faith. We enforce the written judgments by speaking God's Word (see chapter 15) and by invoking his presence through praise. Speak to demonic forces just as you would to people, telling them in the name of the Lord what they must or must not do. Where do you see Satan's kingdom ruling in your local or national government? Over what office or sphere of influence? By faith declare it to be bound in Jesus' name. Then invoke that name as overruling authority there. For instance, you may pray something like this:

I acknowledge and invoke the overruling power of Jesus Christ over our legislature today. In his almighty name, I resist and bind the forces of Satan which are trying to influence legislation that is contrary to the express will of God. I invoke the power and influence of God's Spirit over those who are making these decisions.

Then fast if necessary, and pray on until you see things change or until you feel free in your heart to stop interceding.

Be aware that sometimes God allows drastic things to happen to bring the church and the nation to their knees. Praise him in that, too. We must acknowledge that even his disciplines and judgments are good and righteous. He does hear us and honor our prayers, but we must leave the results to him. Our part is to persevere and pray.

No matter how powerful or entrenched the enemy may seem, don't come at this with a heavy, discouraged, or fearful attitude. We serve a mighty, awesome, triumphant God. Like the monks, perform your dance. The joy of the Lord is our strength (see Neh. 8:10).

When our son, Buddy, was nine years old, he began having trouble sleeping. He was scared. He told us someone was in his room, talking to him—someone he couldn't see. He was a pretty dramatic little guy, so we didn't take him too seriously at first. We gave him some comforting hugs and left the night-light on. But when this went on for a couple of nights, we decided to take him seriously after all. We went into his room, explained to the devil that this child belonged to God, and then told him to leave. Buddy went peacefully to sleep.

But the very next night it happened again. At that point, we explained to our son whom he belongs to and whose kingdom and power protect him. "You are of God, little children, and have overcome them because He who is in you is greater than he who is in the world" (1 John 4:4). We told him to declare it himself. He sat up in his bed and did it, with surprising conviction and authority. And that was the end of that problem.

Authority is not only a defensive weapon, as it was with our son, but is an aggressive and powerful one that enforces God's will in matters of intercession. It is a method of rulership, to be used by mature and wise people. Here is a sample prayer:

In the name of Jesus and through the power of his cross and resurrection, I take authority over Satan's dominion in this matter. I declare that Jesus Christ is victor over all the works of darkness and that his will shall be done here and now.

In this way Jesus, living in his earthly body, the church, rules in the midst of his enemies (see Ps. 110:2). It is our responsibility to see that his will is done on earth through sensitive spiritual discernment, authoritative intercession, and persevering spiritual warfare.

This Present Wackiness

Picture the scene as one fine day in Louisiana, the police try to stop a suspicious-looking car that instead of pulling over, speeds off into the woods and hits a tree. Then the people start piling out like one of those clown acts in the circus. They just keep coming and coming, twenty of them, including five in the trunk. To add a further bizarre touch, they are all stark naked. Their leader, a preacher, explains that they are fleeing from the devil. On the way they have decided their clothes are demon-possessed, so they have abandoned them along with three cars that have run out of gas. The preacher is arrested, and the rest escape into the woods.[24]

This kind of thing is both funny and incredibly sad. These folks were obviously terrified, and their example can make people think that all spiritual warfare is nutty. It isn't; however, it does lend itself to all manner of strange and extravagant behaviors.

For some Christian thrill-seekers, it is a sort of glorified Dungeons and Dragons game in which the imagination is fired and emotions run high with a perceived sense of power. Some prayer groups spend more time yelling at the devil and generally throwing up dust than declaring God's sovereignty and power. Some folks who are really on the fringe have even tried beating the devil out of each other, a dangerous and futile practice that can land its victims in the hospital and its practitioners in jail.

While we believe in the reality of demonic spirits, we don't for a moment blame Satan or demonic powers for all of society's woes. Much of the ugliness in the world is caused by rebellious people who simply have chosen to sin (see James 1:14). We need to figure out the difference and then be careful not to go off the deep end. To do this, we can ask God for the spiritual gift of discernment. Our greatest protection from error is always the Word of God.

Both theology and demonology consist of gathering facts and formulating doctrines from Scripture. Trouble starts when we form doctrines and practices based on experience without checking to see if they line up with the Scriptures. These doctrines can become laced with enough error to make them dangerous—exciting, but dangerous.

They also raise unrealistic expectations, as in the case of the fledgling missionary who gets off the plane at his new station and immediately binds Satan and every spirit in the country (like lassoing a whole herd of cattle all at once), then proceeds on the assumption that this has been successfully done. His first encounter with the local witch doctor may be an eye opener.

Our young missionary will learn firsthand that spiritual warfare is not a mind game. It is a real war in which we wrestle with a determined enemy and in which people sometimes get hurt. We must be determined, too. There are some demonic powers that can be uprooted only by persistent prayer and fasting (see Matt. 17:21).

If you answer the battle cry, don't be surprised if you get dents in your armor and accumulate some spiritual bandages. But ultimately you will win. And because of your courage and perseverance, many will be saved from a fate worse than death.

You don't need to be afraid. If you've done your best to fulfill God's ifs, you're on winning ground. You can face

God with faith, and the devil with confidence. You will come to rejoice in the struggle even when it gets rough, because you'll understand that you're making inroads into an evil kingdom and shaking up its leadership.

When we took our musical *Come Together* into Britain, we realized we would get into a serious spiritual battle because Satan fears nothing more than unity in the church—and that's what the presentation was all about. We knew we were right when a friend called and said, "I woke up at three o'clock this morning hearing the Lord say, 'Pray for the Owenses; the devil is very angry with them.' I don't want you to be afraid, but you should be careful to keep one another covered." We laughed out loud, not because we don't take the devil seriously, but because we were so glad we were upsetting him and his kingdom and making a difference in the world.

We had the same sort of message as we toured with *If My People.* God told us that he would bless powerfully but that it would cost us more than we knew. To this day we carry physical, emotional, and spiritual scars from these battles. But there are churches functioning today that had their beginnings in the teaching of those musicals. Roger Forster, founder of the March for Jesus events, says that the marches had their beginnings when the British took our musical *Come Together* to the streets. Following that, multiplied thousands of people were saved and taught to worship, minister, and intercede.

Interceding spiritual warriors should always focus on their wonderful, powerful God rather than on the satanic. Nevertheless, there is a need to be constantly alert. Satan has more than one arrow in his quiver, and he uses them all. He tempts us not only with the sins of the world and the flesh but with the age-old pull of idolatry—the occult—which we will examine in detail in the next chapter.

Thinking It Over

1. Do you feel you understand your biblical responsibility and authority in this warfare?
2. What does it mean to identify with Christ? (Andrew Murray's *Covenants and Blessings*[25] is a real help in understanding this subject.)
3. What does it mean to "dethrone the devil"? Does the idea intimidate or challenge you?
4. As a soldier of Christ, do you foresee any needed changes in your focus on your worldly affairs? What are they and how will you deal with them?
5. How do you "bind the enemy"?
6. What are some protective measures you can take to avoid "spiritual wackiness"?
7. What do you think should be your main focus in spiritual warfare?

Suggestions for Prayer

- Pray the following Scriptures, claiming these truths for yourself: Romans 6:11; Galatians 2:20; James 4:7.
- Ask God to show you every relationship and practice that might hold you back from being a good soldier of Christ. Then submit these things to his control.
- Use binding prayer over satanic things affecting your community or nation.

14

The Occult

It is evening in a small city in England as our friend Jean Darnall addresses a large home meeting. As she stands in front of the enormous fireplace in the vicarage, she is aware of a big black dog stretched out on the hearth. He belongs to an exotic lady, all in black, who sits in the front row. As Jean begins to speak, the dog starts to growl. She tries to ignore him. He raises his head and stares at her, growling louder. His attitude is threatening, but nobody moves a muscle to stop him. Finally Jean says, "I think this dog is unhappy with me. We both might be more comfortable if he were somewhere else. Would you mind removing him?"

With a malevolent glance at Jean, the lady in black stands, collars the dog, and flounces out of the house. The vicar looks miserable and Jean is baffled. She finishes her message feeling that she has made a huge mistake but is unable to figure out what it is.

After the meeting the vicar says, "Oh dear, I wouldn't have had all that happen for the world. It's very awkward."

"What do you mean?" Jean asks.

"Well, you see, she's a very special lady," says the vicar. "Actually, she's a spiritist medium who is such a help in my healing ministry."

Talk about putting the fox in the henhouse! As Jean and her husband minister to the vicar, they find he doesn't know one spiritual kingdom from another. If it's spiritual, he thinks, it must be God. As they patiently teach him from the Word, he is appalled. No wonder, he says, that so many weird things have been happening to him and his family and his church. Later they all try to minister to the medium, but she will have none of it. Thoroughly outraged, she leaves the church and takes with her a load of oppression.

The Occult in Our Nation

Amazingly, many Christians, sometimes through ignorance, are involved in the occult. They are unaware of its subtleties. They don't recognize it when they see it, understand its dangers, or know how to combat it. But they need to learn because God hates it.

In the Old Testament God took drastic action to keep his people free of occult things so they wouldn't pollute the land with satanic wickedness. His judgments were catastrophic: idolaters, astrologers, mediums, and witches were stoned to death.

God killed King Saul, a man he had earlier anointed, "for his disobedience . . . and because he had consulted a medium, and did not ask the Lord for guidance" (1 Chron. 10:13–14 TLB). He also warned Babylon, a heathen nation, that because of its occult sins he would bring terrible judgment. No supernatural powers could help; their astrologers and prognosticators would burn up like stubble (see Isa. 47:13–14). God told Israel that if they inquired of idols instead of him, he would rush down upon them like fire and devour them (see Amos 5:4–8). That's an extreme reaction from a God who means business and who means to be obeyed.

He means business with us too. He says that we are to ask only him for spiritual wisdom. If we do, he will give it to us liberally (see James 1:5).

"Well now, hold on," you may say. "Do you really believe that just having my horoscope done is going to irritate the Lord?"

Yes, we do. The early church understood this, and Christians who had practiced "curious, magical arts" confessed their sin and burned their books and charms publicly (see Acts 19:18–20). No matter that the paraphernalia was expensive; they feared God, and keeping their relationship right with him was all that mattered.

Acceptance of occult practices may be a determining factor in our fate as a nation. God says that anyone who practices magic or calls on spirits for aid or is a charmer, medium, or wizard is an object of horror and disgust to the Lord, and it is because the nations do these things that the Lord will displace them (see Deut. 18:10–12). For the sake of the soul of our nation, this is a grave and crucial matter about which intercessors must be faithful to watch and pray.

There is an amazing depth and breadth of occult influence in American society. Its greatest danger is that much of it seems so innocent at first.

Take the case described in *The Exorcist*, the first in a line of major occult-horror books and movies. In this story, based on a case history, a young girl becomes grossly demon possessed. Her downward spiral begins with a Ouija board. Unfortunately, these spirit boards, by which people try to communicate with the dead or with disembodied spirits, have been a popular parlor game in many homes for years. But they aren't a game to God.

We know of junior high schoolgirls attempting levitation and seances at their slumber parties. They usually do it in ignorance, and amid giggles and glasses of pop it all seems harmless. But it isn't.

Housewives sit over their morning coffee, reading their daily horoscopes in the local newspaper and offending the God who has commanded them not to do it.

Mystics, occult "prophets," mediums, and psychics are popular guests on television talk shows. Many have special telephone numbers which listeners can call, for a fee, to receive advice and thus bring the doctrines of devils right into their homes.

A Gallup poll shows that one fourth of Americans are involved in some form of the New Age movement, which is nothing more than a modern name for an ancient error. It has some worthy goals: get in tune with nature, clean up the air, save the planet. It brings encouragement to discouraged people by teaching them that they simply haven't discovered their limitless human potential—and that may often be true. But then the other shoe drops, and they are dazzled by the revelation that each of them is actually God!

The spiritual goal of New Age is the deification of humanity and the entire created order. There is no Creator God, no fixed moral code, no guilt, no judgment. Perfection of humanity comes not through repentance and redemption but through a sudden, staggering evolutionary transformation called the "quantum leap," whereby humankind will become entirely recreated and freed from old evils.

Many New Agers, following the lead of celebrities seeking repentance-free religion, have adopted reincarnation: If at first you don't succeed, try, try again . . . and again . . . and again. These teachings of reincarnation and the deification of humanity bring us back to the original lie: "You will not surely die. . . . You will be like God" (Gen. 3:4–5).

There are also many New Agers who consult trance channelers, or spirit mediums. Some of them claim to receive instruction from extraterrestrial guides who visit them via UFOs. Some are so zoned out, they probably believe it!

Though not all New Agers believe the same doctrines, they are united by a mystical, occult worldview that is permeating our society, especially through our entertainment media and educational systems, both of which powerfully influence our young people.

Guarding the Children

There is a program in progress on the educational TV channel, featuring a colorful classroom full of eight- to ten-year-olds. They lie flat on their backs, eyes closed, quiet as mice. An attractive young man with a soothing voice is leading them through their initial experience in relaxation techniques. They have just finished deep-breathing exercises and are now busy "imaging."

"You are floating over a lovely green valley," he tells them and describes a glorious place of trees and flowers and flowing water. "Look around you. Isn't it wonderful? You are happy and peaceful and completely relaxed. No worries, no fears." He gives them a moment to visualize the scene. "Now you are standing among the flowers. Suddenly you see someone coming toward you, a beautiful new friend. You feel as if you've known this friend all your life, and you are so glad to see one another!

"Now picture this," he goes on. "Your friend is reaching out and offering you a gift. It's something—anything—you've always wanted. You are holding it with your hands. Think about it. Look at it. It makes you so happy!" (He makes no suggestion as to what the gift might be.)

"As you look at the gift, you are slowly moving away. Now you look back and your friend is gone. Then the valley is gone, and you are gently moving back into your body in this room. Now," he says softly, "you can open your eyes." They open their eyes and lie quietly for a few seconds, then slowly begin to sit up.

"Do you see how calm you feel, how peaceful it is in here?" their mentor asks. "Remember how keyed up you were when you came in with all your energy ricocheting off the walls? Well, now you've focused that energy inward and centered yourselves. You are truly relaxed. And remember, you can do this anytime you feel tense or nervous, and you'll become as calm as you are now." And it is true, you've never seen a more subdued bunch of kids. Then, slowly, questioning hands go up, but before the mentor has time to answer questions, the show is over.

It would be fascinating to know how following sessions might go. How do you suppose the relationship with the "new friend" might develop? Lots of possibilities for young minds here, don't you think? By the way, guess who sponsored the program? *We* did—you and I—through the tax-supported National Endowment for the Arts.

There is also the problem of occult teaching, not just on television but permeating the public schools. The United States now offers to many public school children courses in eastern meditation ("relaxation techniques") and the calling up of demon guides ("old souls" or "wise

150

old teachers") through imaging and listening to "inner voices."

Be alert. If you find occult practices such as this in your children's classrooms, see that either the practices or your children are removed. Don't think these teachings are nonsense and not worthy of notice. They are an alluring and exciting spiritual trap and seriously anti-Christ. None of us can afford to make them a part of our lives.

For our older children, some universities offer courses in witchcraft, ESP, clairvoyance, and transcendental meditation. This last technique may be called by different names, but it's still the same old eastern practice leading to altered states of consciousness. New Age variations of transcendental meditation are religious, no matter what its practitioners may say. The writings of Maharishi Mahesh Yogi, one of the earlier and more influential of its teachers, called these techniques "a path to God . . . a most powerful form of prayer; a way that will enable men to find their God within themselves."

Here are religious movements without a Creator God and without redemption, whose proponents are laboring to have all references to God forbidden in the same schools in which their own doctrines of spiritual transcendence are being openly taught under various euphemisms.

Beware too of transpersonal psychology that encourages psychic phenomena. Although this has been labeled with respectable scientific terminology by some universities, it is devilish.

Ron Valle, associate dean of the Graduate School of Consciousness Studies at John Kennedy University, points out that . . . the roots of transpersonal thinking are ancient indeed: . . . (it) has its deeper roots in . . . Zen and Tibetan Buddhism, yoga and Hindu thought, Sufism, Christian mysticism, Taoism, mystical Judaism and the views of Native American cultures.[26]

Nations that permit or promote these practices bring down the wrath of God upon their own heads. Not only do they have God's wrath to fear but the one they have turned to is already rewarding them with the harvest of their sin: violence, disease, and destruction.

One of the most serious results of the church's lack of awareness, intercession, and action has been our failure to guard our children against occult powers and the rituals of blatant Satanism. We know children who were taken to satanic rites by a high school baby-sitter. There they were sexually abused and then terrified into silence. When their parents discovered what happened and reported it to the police, they learned that their case was only one among hundreds. In fact, according to a Gallup poll, Satanism is the fastest-growing religion in America.

We need to build strong buffer zones of intercession and spiritual warfare around all our children and be personally aware and involved with all that concerns them. Jesus told us centuries ago that Satan is a deceiver who comes to steal, kill, and destroy (see John 10:10). Nothing has changed. Young and old, Christian and pagan alike, the devil hates us all.

This is a good time for a checkup on occult practices in your life—hangovers from the past, perhaps, such as witchcraft, necromancy, sorcery, astrology, or communion with spirits. You can repent of them and renounce them right now. Then destroy any paraphernalia such as charms, books, and horoscope charts. There will never be a better time to make sure this is taken care of once and for all and to be set free.

When we play around in any enemy territory, we play by his rules, and he will take quick and terrible advantage of us. But as long as we give no "place to the devil" (Eph. 4:27), we are on solid and safe ground. A praying, fasting church, moving in purity and spiritual authority, is fully equipped and qualified to wage powerful warfare against the demonic doctrines of the occult. For the sake of our nation, we must do it now.

Thinking It Over

1. Has reading this chapter changed your thinking in any way regarding occult practices? How?
2. Do you think the church, by and large, is aware of the seriousness and danger of occultism? If not, what are the negative results of that unawareness?
3. How do occult practices in the nation affect God's dealings with us? How might they influence local or national government?
4. Have you checked out what your children are being taught in school regarding meditative and imaging techniques? How can you best do that?
5. If you find occult–New Age teaching in the public schools, what practical steps might you take to stop it?
6. Have you repented for and broken with all past and present occult practices?

Suggestions for Prayer

- Repent of and renounce any occultism in your life. (A good idea: Destroy any occult paraphernalia you possess.)
- Ask for spiritual discernment to keep you sensitive and sensible in dealing with occult influences in your community.
- Pray against occult influences in the lives of the leaders in our government and the mind molders of our society.

The Spiritual Armory

"All right, people, we're at war!" the general shouts as he reviews a throng of new recruits. Packed onto the parade ground of the army base, they shiver in the midnight cold. Jerked from their beds by a besieged and desperate military, they are still in civilian clothes, confused, unprepared, and unarmed.

"We're being invaded from all sides by a well-organized, well-armed enemy who is moving fast," the general informs them. "This is no foreign battle; this is here, now. *Your* homes, *your* families, are already under attack." Even as he speaks, they see the first flare of rockets and hear the sound of artillery.

The initial babble of alarm turns quickly to a roar of outrage. Spines stiffen, fists clench, adrenaline flows. They look expectantly at the general, waiting for orders, for arms.

"All right!" he roars. "About face!"

The massive gates of the compound swing open.

"Now!" shouts the general to his weaponless recruits. "Go get 'em!"

Like these fictional recruits, we have been thrown, unsuspecting and unprepared, into a cosmic war. But unlike the fictional general, God has not called us into battle without armor, arms, and instruction. He has given us powerful and holy equipment for the battle. First there is protective armor, then an arsenal of spiritual weapons and prayer techniques, some of which we've already discussed, such as declaring our identification with Christ, speaking the word of authority, and binding and loosing. But there are a few more, and we need to learn to use them all if we are to be dynamic intercessors.

The Armor

Protection, that's what we need! God has tailor-made an armor for intercessors:

Wear the whole armor of God that you may . . . resist evil . . . and . . . stand your ground. Take . . . truth as your belt, righteousness [as] your breastplate, the Gospel of peace . . . on your feet, salvation as your helmet and in your hand the sword of the Spirit, the Word of God. . . . Take faith as your shield, [to] quench every burning missile [of] the enemy. . . . Pray at all times . . . keeping alert and persistent as you pray for all Christ's [people].

Ephesians 6:13–18 PHILLIPS

Do the verse. Speak God's Word. Put the armor on by faith. When your feet hit the floor in the morning, say, *In the name of Jesus I put the helmet of his salvation over my mind, and the breastplate of his righteousness over my heart. I gird myself with his truth. I take his Word as*

155

my sword, and I shield myself with faith in the Son of God, who lives in me and is greater than any other power that exists. In other words, put on the Lord Jesus Christ (see Rom. 13:14).

However, you don't have to go through the whole list every time you have a battle to fight. Simply say to the enemy, "I stand here covered by Jesus Christ the Lord. In his name I assume his authority over you." Then tell him what he must do, and keep at it until he does it!

We need protection against our own natures as well as against Satan. We are vulnerable wherever we are sinful. Keep yourself armored daily against sin this way:

- *Submit* yourself to God (see James 4:7).
- *Consider* yourself dead to sin and alive to God through Jesus Christ (see Romans 8).
- *Claim* the righteousness of Jesus Christ as your own (see Romans 8).

The Holy Spirit will then progressively impart the righteousness already imputed to you through Christ. This is powerful protection.

More Weapons for Warfare

Let's examine some additional warfare weapons: the sound of praise; the sword of the Word; the blood of the Lamb and the Word of our testimony; the power of petition.

The Sound of Praise

Nepal is the world's only nation where Hinduism is the state religion. Its atmosphere is dense with the influence of a million gods. Religious proselytizing is illegal. Nevertheless, an intrepid YWAM team went in determined to tell people about Jesus. They soon found that no one would even listen. It looked as if they would have to get arrested to get some attention. They were out of ideas and discouraged.

Then one morning they held their praise and worship time outside on their rooftop patio. As they sang their praise to God, they heard voices drifting up from the street below and took a look over the edge. There was a crowd of Nepalese neighbors looking back at them.

"What are you doing?" somebody called up to them.

"We're worshiping God," they replied.

The crowd buzzed a while among themselves, talking it over. Then the spokesman called back up, "We've never heard people sing to their God like that before. Come down and tell us about him."

The Hindus, accustomed to repetitive chants and mantras, wanted to know what kind of god could evoke such joyous, spontaneous song in his worshipers. The YWAMers were delighted to tell them.

Their songs of praise, lifting up the name of the Lord and invoking his presence, became a formidable force that broke through the spiritual powers that kept the Nepalese from receiving the gospel. "Let the high praises of God be in their mouth, And a two-edged sword [the Word of God] in their hand. . . . To bind their kings with chains, And their nobles with fetters of iron; To execute on them the written judgments—*This honor have all His saints*" (Ps. 149:6, 8–9, emphasis added).

Praise, either sung or spoken, literally invites God's presence and binds spiritual kings and destroys strongholds. For example, look again at the siege of Judah as King Jehoshaphat calls that great fast before the battle. Then he devises one of the more amazing military strategies on record: He sends the singers out in front of the army. (Being in the choir in those days was a real adventure!) The victory comes when the singers begin to sing and praise God. *Then* the Lord sends ambushments against the enemy armies and they destroy one another. Praise goes before the Lord's people like a consuming fire.

The Sword of the Word

Jesus uses the sword of the Word as his personal weapon of choice when Satan goads him to demonstrate his divinity (see Matt. 4:1–11). When Satan suggests he turn stones into bread, Jesus doesn't bluster or debate; he simply reminds him, "It is written: 'Man does not live on bread alone, but on every word that comes from the mouth of God'" (v. 4 NIV).

When Satan proposes that Jesus jump off a pinnacle of the temple to see if the angels will rescue him before he hits the street, Jesus reminds him again, "It is also written: 'Do not put the Lord your God to the test'" (v. 7 NIV).

When Satan offers Jesus the kingdoms of the world in exchange for his worship, Jesus has had enough. He says, "Away from me, Satan! For it is written: 'Worship the Lord your God, and serve him only'" (v. 10 NIV). There is no answer from the devil. He has heard "the written judgments" and there is nothing left to say. He simply goes away (see v. 11).

Jesus used "God's mighty weapons, not those made by men, to knock down the devil's strongholds" (2 Cor. 10:4 TLB). God's weapons can pull down strongholds for us too. They may be spiritual, political, or personal, anything in which Satan has gained a foothold. One of his most debilitating personal strongholds is condemnation. As one lady observed wryly, "For most of my life,

I thought guilt was one of the five senses." Sadly, she is not alone in that misconception.

Satan uses vague feelings of unworthiness or condemnation to rob us of faith and power and to make us feel unworthy to petition God or intercede for others. The Holy Spirit, on the other hand, clearly pinpoints problems so we can confess, repent, and accept our cleansing. Guilt over sins already forsaken is not from God. He never condemns a repentant heart.

The Blood of the Lamb and the Word of Our Testimony

The blood of the Lamb and the word of our testimony, two powerful weapons against condemnation or any other satanic ploy, are listed together in Revelation 12:11. The "word of our testimony" is our confession of faith (see Heb. 3:1; 10:23). When condemnation hits us, or whenever we need to assert authority over Satan, we simply declare to him what the blood of Jesus Christ has done for us:

- I am cleansed from sin and have perfect peace with God.
- I belong to Christ; I am his possession.
- I am under his protection.
- I am acting under his authority.

The enemy may resist that authority, but if we know our rights and persevere, he has to give way.

We actually make these confessions out loud. They increase our faith and declare our freedom from bondage and satanic bullying. Speak them often—they really work!

The Power of Petition

- Ask and you shall receive (see John 16:24).
- He will listen to us when we ask him for anything in line with his will (see 1 John 5:14–15).
- You have not because you ask not. You ask and do not receive, because you ask amiss (see James 4:3).

Ask and you shall receive . . . usually. As I was teaching at a Christian women's conference, one of the organizers asked for a private word with me. This was the kind of gung-ho lady who attends every Christian convention she can find. In her two or three years as a believer, she had heard all the great motivational speakers on prosperity, faith, power praying, and evangelism, and she was, in her words, "on fire for Jesus." She was in a fever of excitement about moving to another city to take the regional director's job, which tentatively had been offered to her by the organization. However, even though she had been fervently petitioning God, things didn't seem to be working out; it was just one frustrating hang-up after another. She asked if I would pray with her that Satan's blockades would be broken and she would be set free to get out there and serve God.

I asked her if she was sure this was the will of God. The zealous lady was amazed at such an elementary question. Of course she knew it was the will of God! Otherwise, why would she be divorcing a perfectly good husband so she could leave town?

Our prayer time quickly became a Bible study. Then I had a chat with the lady's leadership, all of whom were unaware of her plans for divorce. These women were wise and sensitive; they recognized that while her zeal was real and her organizational gifts exceptional, there were massive gaps in her understanding of basic Christian life and conduct. With love and compassion, her leadership withdrew her from her place of authority until she had gone through extensive discipling.

In this lady's case, she had all along been receiving God's answer to her petition for promotion. To keep her from self-destructing, he was telling her no.

Petition is the most formidable spiritual weapon we have. It brings heaven to bear on our situation. It brings us help, solutions, and revelation. "Call to Me," God says, "and I will answer you, and show you great and mighty things, which you do not know" (Jer. 33:3). However, when we ask amiss, as did the woman in the story, we are in for a spiritual blockade. It can happen to veteran intercessors, too. It therefore behooves us to find the will of God so we can ask in faith—and get results.

Our chief source of revelation is, of course, the Word of God. Not only is it a formidable weapon, it is the most important faith-building, error-avoiding tool God has given us. There are no shortcuts here. If you've never done any disciplined Bible study, start with Bible classes at your church. Then try the Navigators' memorization system or take a Bible school extension course.

There are times, of course, when we can't find scriptural revelation on the details for a here-and-now problem. James 1:5 says that if we need wisdom, we can ask God for it and he will give it to us. Here are the directional arrows we watch for:

- God's revealed will through his Word
- Inner conviction
- Confirmation of that conviction through trusted counsel
- Circumstances (open doors and divine appointments)

Jimmy and I look for *all* of these before we move. This requires praying and listening. And it requires patience.

Thinking It Over

1. Have you tried putting on your spiritual armor using the method discussed in this chapter? What results have you seen? Do you feel this practice will become a regular part of your life?

2. Do you think you have a good grasp of the biblical teaching on spiritual weapons? Could you explain them to someone else? What examples do you know that demonstrate their effectiveness?

3. Do you see the connection between praise and the Word of God as a means of spiritual warfare? Have you had occasion to try them?

4. What do you need to know in order to speak and ask in faith?

5. What are some directional arrows leading us to God's will? How are these indicators working for you?

Suggestions for Prayer

- Put your armor on.
- Claim the benefits of Jesus' blood.
- Use the spiritual weapons you have been studying to tackle some ungodly problem in your community or in the nation. (Make it an ongoing project.)
- Take time to listen. God may want to give you some strategy that will help solve the problem.
- Pray for local government officials.

16

Attitude Counts

Even though we know all about our spiritual weapons and how to use them, if our attitudes are wrong, it's possible to fast and pray, bind and loose, and all those good things and still find ourselves flat-out and feet-up on the battlefield. One of the hardest and most important attitudes is the patience to wait on God.

Patience: Waiting for God's Will

A dramatic turning point in our lives came when God showed us he had something new for us to do. But he also showed us we didn't know how to do it yet. In fact, we didn't even know what it was, so we were not to write anything more until we learned. Well, that didn't sound too bad at first; we needed a little vacation. But our vacation from writing went on for a year and a half.

Although just enough other work came knocking on our door to keep food on the table, we felt strongly that we were not to look for work; our job was to wait on God. Since writing was our major source of income, however, by the end of that year and a half we had reached the bottom of the money barrel but still had no clue as to what God wanted us to do. By the time we had to sell the piano to pay the bills, we were getting panicky. Still we waited . . . and wondered. Had we heard right? Were we crazy? (By the way, all this was done with the knowledge and encouragement of our pastor and fellow church board members. Still, the thought did occur: Maybe we're *all* crazy!)

Finally the breakthrough came when our pastor, Jack Hayford, casually remarked over Sunday dinner, "Maybe God wants you to write a musical about our church." Then he laughed.

Jimmy didn't. Instead he thought, That's it! A musical not about our church but about what God has been teaching our church for the last year and a half. Out of all this came a musical called *Come Together,* which spawned another called *If My People,* followed by *The Witness* and several others. From the time of waiting and praying and listening sprang ministry more far-reaching and powerful than all our former ministry combined.

Our family never missed a meal or failed to pay our bills while all this was going on. If that had happened, we would have known we had heard wrong and immediately done something to remedy things. We were not people looking for an excuse to loaf. God's attitude toward laziness is, "If a man will not work, he shall not eat" (2 Thess. 3:10 NIV). We were willing; we were just waiting for our specific path, and we found it.

If the church will wait on the Lord until we hear his instructions, we will be dramatically more effective in intercessory prayer and action. Ephesians 2:10 sheds clear light on this: "For we are God's own handiwork

(His workmanship), recreated in Christ Jesus, born anew that we may do those good works which God pre-destined (planned beforehand) for us, taking paths which He prepared ahead of time, that we should walk in them living the good life which He prearranged and made ready for us to live" (AB).

Not just any good works . . . but *those* good works.

Not just any paths . . . but *those* paths.

Not just any life . . . but *that* life . . . planned, prepared, prearranged.

Finding a need and trying to fill it isn't always the best plan. God has promised to bless only what is in his will. There is a master plan (prepared by the Master), and we need to find our place in it as we intercede with our prayers and lives. So we have to learn to wait, watch, and listen.

Some things are plainly part of our prayer assignment, such as family and church. We also have a scripturally given prayer responsibility for our government. The most telling way to fulfill these assignments is to ask God to bring specific situations and people to our attention. Then we will pray his prayers in his will.

To make sure you are hearing God's voice in your heart, begin by practicing James 4:7, which says, "Therefore submit to God. Resist the devil and he will flee from you." Our friend Joy Dawson uses this Scripture to teach a powerful three-step procedure:

- *Resist the devil and he will run from you.* In Jesus' name forbid Satan and demonic powers to speak to you.
- *Submit yourself to God.* Tell him you are submitting your will, your opinions, and your desires to him.

• *Wait and listen patiently.* God may bring someone's name or face into your mind. It will keep coming back, nagging at you until you pray.

When you are confident that you are praying in God's will, you will be able to ask in faith and speak with authority.

You may say, "I feel certain that what I'm asking for is in the will of God, but I don't see any progress with my problem. Is that a blockade? What now?"

Maintain your attitude of authority, praise, and patience. The Lord isn't under bondage to the pressures of time, and he's never in a hurry. Once you know you have the mind of God, just keep the faith! You're in a warfare that is fought skirmish by skirmish. Your opposition is real and your job is to stand fast.

Speaking of the Devil

If we do not maintain the proper attitudes in spiritual warfare, we will find ourselves in deep and murky waters. Although we may not understand why, we are told to follow spiritual protocol in dealing with our satanic enemy. While we may operate with utmost boldness, arrogance is out of place. It is unscriptural and unwise to use derision or scorn when speaking of or to the devil. God says not to do it, so we don't. People who encourage you to adopt this attitude are either uninformed or disobedient to the Word. Jude, in warning the church about false teachers, says, "Their dreams lead them to . . . insult celestial beings. In contrast, when the archangel Michael was in debate with the devil, disputing the possession of Moses' body, he did not presume to condemn him in insulting words, but said, 'May the Lord rebuke you'" (Jude 8–9 NEB).

Peter also says that false teachers are reckless and headstrong and insult celestial beings, while angels, with all their strength and power, never employ insults when seeking judgment against them before the Lord (see 2 Peter 2:10–11).

We don't need to employ abusive words against the enemy. All we need is the knowledge of our authority in union with Christ's power. Our method is to refer Satan to Calvary; he knows he lost the battle there. We refer him to the empty tomb and to the ascension; he knows he was stripped of his authority then. Now he knows that we know it, and that puts things on a different footing.

However, while it's true that we're identified with Christ in his authority and righteousness, we can't use that as a haven to harbor deliberate, known sin. If we try it, devils will laugh in our faces when we challenge them. So before we charge in with bared bayonets, we'd better have the humility to check—often—for our vulnerable areas. We need to keep short accounts with God, turning quickly to confession and repentance. To be able to say with Jesus, "Satan, you have nothing on me" (see John 14:30) is to be in the position of safety and power.

Spiritual warriors need balanced attitudes: boldness through our authority in Christ, and humility to keep us aware of our vulnerability and total dependence on him. Jesus meant it when he said, "Apart from me you can do nothing" (John 15:5 NIV).

Boldness is an offensive weapon that preaches the Word and wins battles. Humility keeps us clinging to Jesus, saves us from spiritual independence, and leads us into the covering of submission.

Submission: For Protection and Correction

Remember this old familiar war-movie scenario? Van Johnson and Robert Taylor are frantically clawing their way through the jungle, heading for cover after setting explosive charges to blow up a strategic enemy bridge. The success of their mission will, of course, determine the entire outcome of World War II. From a safe distance they stop to watch the explosion. Nothing happens. They claw their way back again. Looking through their field glasses, they find the problem: The fuse has gone out.

Van loses the coin toss, so he goes back to relight the fuse. By this time, massive enemy troops are approaching the bridge from the other side. Van's chances of remaining undetected are nil. His only protection is Robert Taylor with his rifle, popping away at the enemy horde. Van, of course, blows up the bridge but, overwhelmed by the enemy's firepower, dies a hero's death.

What the poor man needed was the covering of a whole platoon of heavily armed soldiers. There are some things you just shouldn't try without the proper protective cover.

No matter how strong or important we may think we are, every one of us needs a covering. We find it in our submission to the church. These are our fellow warriors. Just as soldiers in battle cover one another with protective fire, so Christians are constantly to shield and defend one another through intercessory prayer and spiritual warfare, keeping alert and persistent as we pray for all Christ's men and women (see Eph. 6:18).

The covering doesn't come automatically; we need the wisdom to ask for it and the humility to submit to it. We need trusted pastors, spiritual mentors, and prayer partners. We need them not only for their help in the heat of battle but for their wise correction, which may save us from many a disaster along the way.

A well-known evangelist took a public and messy fall. He made a public "repentance," too. We saw the hearts of many leaders go out to him; they wanted to see him restored. So did his denomination, which asked him to step down from public ministry for a year and serve quietly under the supervision and counsel of his superiors. He refused. His church would fall apart without him, he said, and besides, he didn't need supervision. So he stayed in the pulpit. Within a short time, down he went again.

Every Christian soldier—even those in positions of high authority—needs the counsel and aid of experienced warrior-leaders. The apostles answered to one another for how they lived, what they taught, and how they ministered. This protected them and the church from error. When Paul and Peter were opposed by other teachers, they submitted to the conclusions of a council of apostles and elders at Jerusalem. If they operated in the attitude of submission to the church, how much more should we?

Because Jimmy and I travel for extensive periods, we're not constantly under the eye of a local body. Instead we have a group of mature, spiritually seasoned men and women—some of whom are on our ministry board and some of whom are pastors—who are only a phone call away. These are the people we counsel with before we make major moves. We are not shy about calling for help or admitting when we are having a hard time hearing God. They pray with and for us and ask God to speak to them on our behalf. Sometimes they call us with advice. We listen carefully. They have given us encouragement, direction, and correction for years. There's no way to tell you how grateful we are for them. "For by wise counsel you can wage your war, and in an

abundance of counselors there is victory and safety"
(Prov. 24:6 AB).

Another word of warning: Know the Word and know
it well. Then you will know when you are receiving
proper leadership and can submit to it confidently. It
will keep you from being victimized by future Jim Jone-
ses and David Koreshes.

Persistence Pays

Be aware that a persistent attitude pays off. For instance, when we tried to sell our house, we ran into all
the usual delays with lenders and escrow companies.
The hassle of getting these folks to communicate with
one another was incredible. Transferring papers between neighboring offices apparently required an act of
Congress. "Slow" was an understatement for our non-
progress. At the same time, an acquaintance of ours was
also selling a house. In the twinkling of an eye, it seemed,
all the papers were signed, the deal was closed, and he
had moved out. "Wait a minute here!" we protested.
"How'd you *do* that?"

"I drove 'em crazy," he said. "I called two or three
times every single day, checking them out. At the end I
parked myself in their offices till they signed the papers
I needed, and then I hand-carried them to the next guy
on the agenda." He smiled smugly. "They couldn't get
rid of me fast enough."

Jesus seemed to recommend a similar method of getting what we need through prayer. His story goes something like this: A man has an unexpected midnight visit
from a friend who is passing through town. The friend
is not only tired but hungry. There's a problem: The cup-
board is bare. Our man rushes over to his neighbor's
house and pounds on the door. When the neighbor, look-

ing cross, sticks his head out the bedroom window, our man asks him for three loaves of bread.

"What's the matter with you?" the neighbor replies rudely. "It's midnight! Can't you see the lights are out? We're all in bed, where all decent people should be. Go away!" And he slams the window shut.

But our man is shamelessly and fearlessly persistent. He pounds on the door and waits for the neighbor's head to pop out again. When it does, he repeats his request. This goes on until the neighbor decides that our man is not going away and that nobody is going to get any sleep until the three loaves of bread are handed over.

Jesus said that although the neighbor wouldn't supply our man out of friendship, because of his persistence he got up and gave him as much as he needed (see Luke 11:5–8). Then Jesus added, "So . . . [it is with prayer], Ask and keep on asking and it shall be given you; seek and keep on seeking and you shall find; knock and keep on knocking and the door shall be opened to you" (v. 9 AB).

Keep on. That's the key. After you have prayed in faith, keep on giving thanks for prayer already heard and answers already on the way. Keep on standing firmly on the promises of God's Word. Then let patience complete its work.

You might pray like this:

God, I bring my request to your remembrance. I thank you that you always hear me and that you're moving in my behalf. I just want you to know that I'm still asking and that I'm still waiting with confidence and peace for you to move—and I'll be back.

This was the attitude of the church in Riga, Latvia, under Soviet domination. A letter was smuggled out to us saying that our music had reached them several years previously and that they had risked doing a performance of *Come Together* in an attempt to unify a divided and demoralized church. They had no idea what kind of response they might receive, but happily the venue was packed. "So the work began," they said.

The second program, *If My People*, followed. This called the people to ongoing intercession for their beleaguered nation. For years they steadfastly prayed and built a wall of righteousness for the land. For years nothing happened. Then when God's time finally arrived, the walls of communism crumbled so fast that the whole world watched in awe.

Soon after the communists were deposed, we went on an outreach to the Balkans and Russia with Loren Cunningham, Peter Iliyn, and other YWAM leaders. In Tallinn, Estonia, and Riga, Latvia, the churches collaborated in big public productions of *If My People*. The performances were emotional and powerful as the people gave thanks, worshiped, and prayed. Then they pledged themselves to keep right on praying for their land and, now that the walls of righteousness had been established, to guard its gates.

Maybe you've been praying for a long time for ungodly government officials or against unrighteous or oppressive laws, without seeing any change. Never give up. Let the perseverance and victory of the people of the Balkans give you courage. God still moves in human affairs, and when the time is right, he does a quick work.

A Matter of Life and Death

One last vital attitude: "They did not love and cling to life even when faced with death" (Rev. 12:11 AB). "I am the resurrection and the life. He who believes in Me, though he may die, he shall live. And whoever lives and believes in Me shall never die" (John 11:25–26).

In Estonia we met people with this attitude; it is the attitude of overcomers. One of the churches in which we ministered there is just down the street from the former KGB headquarters, where many of the people were imprisoned and tortured. But they came back out and kept on going, knowing that their lives were on the line. This is what Christianity is all about: It is a faith so strong, an eternal future so sure, that there is no risk in laying down our lives in life intercession, for there is no death for the believer in Christ.

Our son, Buddy, testified to that when, in one of his less-brilliant teenage moves, he and a friend went on a hike and took a shortcut through a long, narrow train tunnel. A train had just come through, so they figured another one surely wouldn't be scheduled for some time. But of course it was.

They had reached the middle of the tunnel when the tracks began to sing. One look behind told them it was too late to go back, so they began to run. Buddy knew within a minute that there was no way they were going to outrun that train. It was so dark that they could see little but the small, bright hole that was the tunnel exit far—too far—ahead.

As the horrendous noise and vibration gained on them by the second, it dawned on Buddy, I am really going to die—right now! The next thought was, Dear God, I'm going to see Jesus. In just a few seconds I'm going to see Jesus! Later he said, "Mom and Dad, that's when I started to get excited."

In spite of his spiritual excitement, his legs kept on running until he and his friend fell into a shallow escape niche carved into the side of the tunnel, where they pressed themselves into the wall while the train slammed past only inches from their faces.

Since they came through relatively unscathed, our first reaction—after kissing Buddy's face off—was to scathe him ourselves. But he had already learned a lesson. He said, "I found out the most important thing in the world in that tunnel; I found out that I really believe all the things I always thought I believed." For those moments at least, Buddy had experienced the certainty of eternal life and freedom from the fear of death. Jesus died to break the bondage Satan holds over us through that fear (see Heb. 2:14–15). When we *know* we have eternal life, we can follow the arrows wherever God leads us, because we have nothing left to fear. When we recognize that, we are liberated.

Prayer of Spiritual Warfare

When we use our armor, wield our weapons, and get our attitudes in order, we are ready for some serious spiritual warfare. Use the following prayer as a jumping-off place from which you can expand upon any and all of these urgent prayer points.

Mighty God, we put on your armor: your salvation, truth, and righteousness. We take the shield of faith to repel Satan's fiery attacks. We lift up your sword—the living Word of God—and with your high praises in our mouths, we come to do battle.

We are the temple of the Holy Spirit, the repository of God's authority in our world. We are the ambassadors of Jesus Christ, who has all power and authority over all the power of the devil. Cleansed and made righteous in God's sight by Jesus' blood, we declare to the powers of darkness that they have no place in us and no power over us.

In Jesus' name we resist the dark spirits that pervert justice and fill our streets with fire and blood. We plead for equal justice for all people in our nation. Lord, replace hatred and violence with your Spirit of peace, compas-

sion, repentance, and reconciliation. In the name of the Lord, we lift up the banner of the kingdom of God and pray for the Spirit of grace over our land.

We resist the deceiving spirits who encourage the slaughter of our unborn children. Give us love, wisdom, and godly strategy as we confront this evil. Bring revelation, conviction, and repentance to those who defend and encourage this terrible sin in our nation.

Lord, break the power of gross immorality and perversion that brings bondage, degradation, and death to thousands of our countrymen. Open the eyes of the spiritually blind. Let them see that truth, life, and real freedom are in Jesus Christ.

We lift your triumphant name over the lying spirits of occultism and idolatry in our land. Expose them with your truth and free those who are entangled in a lie. Protect the minds of your people from these deceptions and keep them pure through your Word.

Lord, you are the Truth. You are the Spirit above all spirits that exist, King above all kings, and Lord of heaven and earth.

We hold a defensive umbrella of prayer over our national decision-makers. Protect them from the enemy's influence. Give them wisdom and courage to make righteous decisions so that your blessing rather than your curse may rest on the country.

We resist the spiritual principalities of darkness that rule in our city. Make us prayer warriors who will persevere until Satan's strongholds crumble.

Renew the church in wisdom, faith, holiness, love, courage, and power so the world may see you in us and believe. Move the whole church to take the whole gospel to the whole world so that we may see in our time the final great harvest that will signal the return of our Lord Jesus Christ!

In that mighty name we pray. Amen.

Thinking It Over

1. What success are you having with waiting on God?
2. What examples of improper attitudes toward satanic powers have you seen or heard? How do you feel about these attitudes? What attitude would you take instead? Why?
3. What do you feel is a proper balance of authority and submission to leadership? Have you seen these principles abused? What are some ways people can know when they are being properly protected or corrected and when they are being victimized?
4. Are you easily discouraged when you don't see immediate answers to prayer? Have you seen successful results from perseverance? How can believers encourage one another in persistent prayer?
5. How do you feel about your own death, or is it a subject you avoid? If you knew death was imminent, what relational fences would you mend? What jobs would you want to complete?

Suggestions for Prayer

- Go back and pray the prayer of spiritual warfare at the end of this chapter.

17

Battle Plans

> The task of the people of God is, as far as possible in sinful society, to reclaim the cosmos for God's created purpose.
>
> Carl F. H. Henry

It's time for action, time for plans and strategies. In this chapter we will examine four plans that will make inroads into the enemy encampment.

Plan 1: First Friday Fasting and Prayer

Nineteen seventy-four. A year of national trauma, disillusionment, and bitterness. The Watergate soap opera in the White House is reaching its denouement, and the country watches and listens with trepidation and sorrow.

On April 30 our church, along with countless others, fasts and prays for the nation at the request of the United States Senate. Our pastor, Jack Hayford, moved by what the Holy Spirit is saying in his own spirit, delivers a prophetic message from God, which says in part, "An era turns on the strength of a day. This day is marked in the annals of eternity, a great turnabout, a day of enormous consequences. An unwritten history of doom and judgment is erased and a new history is being written. The powers of the heavens are being shaken. This is a day of great scattering and confusion among the enemy."

A prophetic utterance is to be judged by whether it comes to pass, and the very next day we begin to see its fulfillment. President Nixon releases the fateful secret tapes, and the rancorous affair is on its way to an end.

From Watergate we learn anew that even people with extraordinary gifts, talents, and a measure of wisdom have a dark side. Our president, Richard Nixon, a man skilled at foreign affairs, is also skilled at subterfuge and revenge. He contributes the term "expletive deleted" to our national vocabulary. Since it was Jesus who said, "Out of the overflow of the heart the mouth speaks" (Matt. 12:34 NIV), this is not the man we thought we knew. His words, whispered in secret, are shouted from the housetops and produce a national cynicism toward government that will plague us for generations to come.

The very existence of those tapes is an enigma. "Why weren't they destroyed early on?" pragmatic Americans ask one another.

"How could someone as bright as Mr. Nixon do something so dumb?" we wonder. "With all the elaborate plans for secrecy and cover-up, how in the world did they manage to get caught?"

"They could make a movie of this thing," we say, "and call it *The Three Stooges Stage a Break-In.*"

It's no wonder they can't cover it up; the hand of God is at work! When he determines to root out corruption, nothing can stop him. "The Most High rules in the kingdom of men, and gives it to whomever He chooses"

(Dan. 4:25). So Richard Nixon steps down and Gerald Ford steps up. At his inauguration President Ford says, "You have not elected me, but I ask you to confirm me with your prayers." A good start.

Almost immediately rain falls in the drought-stricken midwest. Drought is one of God's curses on a sinful nation, while rain in season is one of his blessings (see Deuteronomy 28). A good sign. In our own state and community, notorious terrorist groups and narcotics rings are uncovered and destroyed, the crime rate drops drastically, and righteous legislation regarding hardcore pornography passes, along with many other victories. Great things begin to happen.

But there is more to Pastor Hayford's prophetic word of April 30. It goes on: "The battle turns today, but the completion is yet to be carried out. There will be other days and other battles. There are mighty victories to be accomplished. The battle is the Lord's. The Lord makes you unconquerable."

At this point Jimmy senses that the Holy Spirit is saying something momentous to him, also: "Because the church of Jesus Christ throughout the country is united in purpose for one day, a great battle is being won. But tomorrow will you still be united? Or will you be scattered again, as you were before?"

Jimmy knows that the war against evil will continue to rage. How long, he wonders, before the church is again summoned to battle with a time of concerted, united intercession and fasting? And who will summon her?

In his spirit the certainty grows: If once a month, on a day designated by major Christian leadership across America, we would gather in our churches for fasting, intercession, and spiritual warfare, we would see major spiritual strongholds crumble and principalities topple. Jimmy asks the Lord, How can such a plan be implemented? The assurance comes: If it's born of the Spirit, he will lead, and leaders of the church will confirm it.

Jimmy approaches Pastor Hayford, who enthusiastically confirms the idea. He tells Jimmy the church will back him in prayer and finances if he will travel and meet with leaders throughout the country. These meetings, accomplished primarily through the help of Dr. Lloyd Ogilvie, then pastor of the First Presbyterian Church of Hollywood, California, now Chaplain of the United States Senate, lead to the Summit Conference of Church Leaders in America.

One hundred and thirty leaders come—heads of denominations and parachurch ministries, media and educational leaders, and other Christian statesmen. Together they pray and strategize as to how to turn the tide of darkness in the nation.

The conference ends with a unanimous resolution designating the first Friday of each month as a day of corporate prayer and fasting across the country. The delegates will urge their constituents to rally and pray for government and other critical areas of societal influence, to pray against injustice and crime, to pray for revival. It is a critical and far-reaching decision. Pat Robertson, who leads a group of religious broadcasters at the conference, says on the 700 Club that he considers this the most important conference of the year in America.

Within a year we see dramatic results: Christians are elected to major political offices; television noticeably cleans up its sex-and-violence routine; the crime rate drops significantly in major cities; there is awakening and spiritual growth in the churches. Even the cynical *Washington Post* declares there is "a new spirit abroad in the land." When the church prays, things change.

Unfortunately for America, after the bicentennial year only a few prayer ministries continue to intercede on behalf of the nation. Although their intercession is powerful and persevering, the gravity of the times demands more. But the church at large loses its sense of urgency and ceases to stand in the gap. As the church's vision for intercession fades, America's morality, honor, and strength fade, too. We face daily the results of that failure as we struggle for our national soul through crisis after crisis.

But the good news is that the church in America is again rallying dynamically to this vital need for united intercession. Prayer ministries are proliferating, and the First Friday movement, for so long existing only as an ember, is again being fanned into flame—and it is spreading rapidly. Intercessors for America reports that five thousand churches in America, as well as tens to hundreds of thousands of believers worldwide, are linked together in the observance of the First Friday Day of Fasting and Prayer. The A.D. 2000 and Beyond movement has now adopted the First Friday observation and is promoting it throughout the world.

Recognizing now that corporate intercession may well determine the future of our country, we suggest that this is the time for pastors and leaders to rise up and urge their people to join intercessors nationwide in reinstituting the first Friday of every month as a day of corporate prayer for our cities and nation. It will be a major force in strengthening our spiritual buffer zones and turning our country around. God knows we have seldom needed it more.

Plan 2: Declaration and Invocation: Lift Your Voice!

Is the average Christian being outprayed by the average adherent of other religions? It's a possibility.

Dee Ann struggled valiantly to fan the flames of her community intercession group. The local pastors in this small Texas town declined to participate, and without their leadership the group disintegrated. At their last meeting one new, unfamiliar intercessor came, enthusiastic and eager to pray for the nation. The tiny remnant was thrilled. Only when she began to read aloud from a strange little book did they realize she was an adherent of Baha'i.

Later Dee Ann and her husband drove along the Dallas expressway, listening as the evening news reported some Christmas-season items. A city had put up a Merry Christmas billboard with a Scripture reference on it; the government ordered it taken down. Another town installed manger scenes in their streets and parks; the government ordered them removed. Santa and his elves were fine, but no Jesus was allowed.

Dee Ann was steaming. How long would it be, she demanded rhetorically of her husband, before the church woke up to what was going on and began to bombard heaven for divine intervention and direction? Didn't *anybody* care enough to commit themselves seriously to prayer?

Just then they noticed a car parked on the side of the expressway, with three men sitting on the ground in front of it, oblivious to the roaring traffic. They were praying. It was obvious that they did this often, because they had brought along their prayer rugs. They were Muslims.

"Well, there you are," Dee Ann's husband responded forlornly. "*Somebody's* praying."

As Pope John Paul II says of the Muslims, "It is impossible not to admire their fidelity to prayer. The image of believers in Allah who, without caring about time or place, fall to their knees and immerse themselves in prayer remains a model for all those who invoke the true God."[27]

As a case in point, take another Dee Ann experience. This time she had asked the manager of a Dallas department store for permission to put up a poster in the store promoting the National Day of Prayer. The answer? "I would *love* to do this, but I just can't. It might cost me my job."

The sad thing is, Dee Ann thought as she trudged toward the exit, she's probably right. I guess Christians really have to be careful about speaking out in public these days. Then, to her chagrin, she saw him—a Muslim, kneeling, forehead to the floor, praying . . . right in the middle of Dillard's furniture department.

This man wasn't afraid of what people might think or do; it was time to honor and invoke Allah and he did. And yet, Dee Ann recognized with shock, Jesus' men and women all over America were either uninterested or undisciplined in prayer or were allowing themselves to be intimidated into silence.

Those things happened less than a couple of years ago during a dry time for intercessors with a burden for prayer for the nation. But things soon began to change. As people like Dee Ann persevered, with or without a prayer group, the call to intercession began to swell and rise like a tide across the country. It even swept into her little Texas town, and people are now interceding there too. As a result of the efforts of these newly roused phalanxes of prayer warriors, along with multitudes of outspoken Christian citizens and the bulldog tenacity of fearless Christian attorneys, the Supreme Court recently came through like champions, restoring many of our free speech rights concerning public religious expression.

We are elated by these changes and grateful to the Court. But these decisions are only a beginning. Vigilant, ongoing prayer for the nation is the watchword. This is a war in the spirit first of all, and if we do not remain dedicated, we will find our freedoms eroded again before we realize what has hit us.

The Muslims can certainly teach us a few things about dedication. They understand and practice invocation. It is a simple form of worship that affects the entire nation in which it is practiced. Oh, the Christian church knows the term; we even name it in our church bulletins, but we don't understand it very well or practice it much—certainly not as effectively as they do.

In Islamic countries the public call to worship goes forth five times a day as loudspeakers carry the voices of the muezzin from the mosques across the cities. And five times a day, as the man in Dillard's did, Muslims kneel, faces to the ground, and out loud and corporately declare the sovereignty of Allah and their allegiance to him and to his prophet, Mohammed.

The result, as you know if you've been to the Middle East, is that you can literally feel the presence and influence of the god who is invoked and enthroned there by the worship of the people. Invocation is worship that declares the reality and power of the one who is being invoked, and is an invitation for him to manifest himself. And he does.

This is a major premise in C. S. Lewis's book *The Last Battle* as the villains, in order to terrify the people, invoke the demon god Tash, never believing for a moment that anything will happen. To their unhappy surprise, Tash not only shows up but devours them. They have discovered an interesting spiritual principle: The spirit that is invoked is the spirit that manifests itself.

So it is for the Christian church: The Lord inhabits, or enthrones himself on, the praises of his people (see Ps. 22:3). In other words, he manifests himself where he is publicly honored and welcomed.

Some churches understand the power of declaration and invocation, although they may not use that terminology. They declare Jesus' sovereignty and invite his manifest presence over their families, churches, cities, and nations. They sing it, say it, and shout it from pulpit and pew. The problem is, they do it only for a few minutes once a week—or twice a week, if the faithful little band who turns out for prayer meeting remembers to practice it.

Meanwhile Islam is practicing it faithfully five times a day, seven days a week. Together. Out loud. Millions of them lifting their voices in concerted declaration and invocation.

We wish that more Christians had these Muslims' devotion and discipline in prayer. Nevertheless, as Pope John Paul II recognizes, "Islam is not a religion of redemption. There is no room for the cross and the resurrection."[28] But while they do not have the truth of Jesus Christ and his redemption, they do have spiritual power. So have many other major religions and occultists and New Agers, who are hotly pursuing false gods and familiar spirits who come where they are invited. This is invocation.

We are in a massive spiritual power-struggle worldwide. The church is learning again to declare Jesus' sovereignty and invoke his presence and power over their nation. This being so, what if three times a day, every day, Christians were to exalt the name of Jesus and declare his sovereignty over their nation? What if they were to do it out loud? Corporately? At home, at school, on the job?

"Well," you ask, "how do we do that?" What if we set a time when Christians could join together spiritually all over their cities to invoke the presence of Jesus there? Let's make it simple: mealtimes. Anytime between the hours of 7:00 and 8:30 in the morning, from

12:00 noon to 1:00 in the afternoon, and from 6:30 to 8:00 in the evening. We could make it part of our mealtime blessing.

Next question: "How do we pray?" *Out loud.* We needn't make a scene, but we need to be vocal. It takes only a few moments. It is short, declarative prayer said with focus, fervor, and faith. For example: *Jesus Christ is the risen Son of the Living God. He has all power in heaven and on earth. Let his will be done on earth as it is in heaven. Amen.*

You may choose to put the name of your family, church, community, city, state, or nation in place of the words *on earth.* Or you can use your own words, so long as you proclaim his identity and his authority in our world.

Christians won't have these prayer disciplines forced upon us, as most Muslims have; we'll be responsible to discipline ourselves. But can't we who have the aid of the Holy Spirit dedicate ourselves to making strong daily invocation an ongoing, lifelong practice? The Muslims do. Can't we do it wherever we are without being self-conscious or embarrassed about it? The Muslims do. Surely we can be as dedicated as they!

If we are, God will hear us. Spiritual powers will hear us, too, and as we persist, there will be cracks in the gates of hell, resulting in revival in our churches and changes in our society.

Plan 3: Praying the Television News

Wouldn't it be wonderful if we had a way to call a multitude of intercessors to immediate alert in times of crisis? Well, we have—and it's right in our living rooms.

Jimmy always looks forward to the TV network news; it has become one of his most intense intercession times.

Recently he realized that there must be a multitude of Christians across the nation whose hearts are touched by the daily parade of catastrophe crossing our screens. If only we were aware of each other, we could pray as a united army. If one shall put a thousand to flight and two, ten thousand (see Deut. 32:30), how many spiritual foes can be routed, and strongholds pulled down, by the simultaneous, authoritative prayers of thousands of intercessors across the nation? We could pray with new faith and boldness, knowing that we are not alone but are many.

Agreeing prayer can bring God's blessing, mercy, and grace to a world in turmoil and pain. It can bring victory in warfare. Great spiritual principalities and powers of evil are not routed by loners but by armies of prayer warriors. And that marvelous last-days technology that God has given to us—the ability to communicate images and sound instantly to the whole world from anywhere on earth via television—may be part of God's plan to summon those vast armies immediately to battle.

One of the great values of television is its immediacy. Consider, for example:

TV: "We take you live by satellite to the Beirut airport, where terrorists have seized hostages." Images flash on the screen. Within moments, prayer warriors are called to battle worldwide.

We pray: "In the overruling name of Jesus we resist the spirits of anarchy and violence that drive these terrorists, and as an army we bind them up. Lord, send your angels to confound the powers of darkness. Protect the innocent. Give wisdom to the authorities." Then we stay with it, following the news flashes and responding in prayer as the Spirit directs, until the episode is brought to an end.

TV: "An attorney for a civil rights advocacy group has asserted today that the First Amendment protects all freedom of speech, even child pornography."

We pray: "O God! Destroy these works of ungodliness in Jesus' name. Defeat the plans of those who corrupt our children! We resist the spirits of perversion and depravity that enslave the innocent and bring your wrath upon our country. Forgive us for our apathy, which has allowed this evil to spread across our nation. Show us what action you want us to take now."

Other typical calls to prayer:

Refugees from a natural disaster or war. Relief efforts are held up by bureaucracy. Speak against those obstacles in prayer. Ask mercy for the bereaved and suffering, and blessing on the rescue efforts.

Continuing violence between Israeli troops and Palestinians. Pray for the peace of Jerusalem (see Ps. 122:6). Persevere in prayer for resolution of the conflict.

Drugs, crime, abortion, corruption in government and in the church, AIDS, poverty, injustice. These things and others are daily brought into our homes as instant calls to prayer. All across the time zones of our nation and our world, an intercessory army can be mobilized to resist the devil and cry out to God.

When Christian leaders are being interviewed, pray for godly wisdom and for fair treatment by the media. It is time to support all God's public men and women with our prayers.

Pray for the news media too, that God will save those who determine its content, or remove those who adamantly use their positions to mock righteousness and promote evil causes.

Think what wonders might be accomplished through the daily, agreeing prayer of thousands of Christians.

Plan 4: Community and National Impact: Prayer Bulletins

"I appreciate whatever influence you have with the Almighty. The good Lord knows I need all the help I can get"—Ted Koppel, news anchor, *ABC Nightline.*

"Thank you for your prayers. We can manage all this only with the continued, prayerful support of God's people. . . . Thank all the folks out there who are praying for us"—Charles Swindoll, president, Dallas Theological Seminary.

"Thank you for advising me of the prayers your members offered during my surgery. It was very much appreciated. Please convey my sincere thanks to your congregation for their concern"—Ted Turner, chairman of the board, Turner Broadcasting System, Inc.

"It is your prayers along with others that really sustain me"—Rabbi Yechiel Eckstein, founder and president, International Fellowship of Christians and Jews.

"Thank you for thinking of me. . . . It is rather rare that I receive a note of prayer, and I am pleased to receive them"—Denise Moreno Ducheny, assemblywoman, California State Legislature.

"Thank you. . . . The Police Department has definitely undergone some difficult periods in recent months and sincerely welcomes your continued prayers and encouragement"—Willie L. Williams, chief of police, Los Angeles Police Department.

"This kind of spiritual support is truly valued by me and my family, and it is important that you know how much I appreciate this gesture. . . . Thank you for your prayers"—Dan Rather, news anchor, *CBS Evening News*.

"Thank you for including me in your prayers. These have been difficult times for me and my family. . . . It is the prayers of my friends at my church, Lake Avenue Congregational in Pasadena, as well as those of many brothers and sisters in Christ personally unknown to me, that have given me strength, resolve and, hopefully, wisdom as well"— Judge Lance A. Ito, Superior Court, Los Angeles, California.

These are only a very few samples of the thick and growing file of thank-you notes from state senators, judges, members of Congress, university presidents, business leaders, local pastors, and nationally and internationally known Christian leaders received by the Church on the Way in response to its weekly *Prayer, Praise and People Report*.

This prayer guide is a powerful, carefully crafted ministry tool that aids the church in its intercession. It is concise. It is wide-ranging. It has variety. It covers every sector of life: all facets of society, all areas of national interest, the needs of the local congregation, the closure of the Great Commission, the welfare of the nations.

Most of all, in obedience to 1 Timothy 2:1, it is positive prayer for those in all places of influence. These people not only need our prayers, they appreciate them. They need to hear from us regularly, not only when they are doing things wrong but when they are doing things right. A little encouragement goes a long way.

This outreach goes beyond prayer and becomes goodwill expressed as the church sends the prayer guide, along with personal letters, to the people for whom it is praying. You have just read a tiny fraction of the responses.

The Church on the Way will be glad to share its resources with you so you can find the people and issues that need your prayers, and will tell you where to find the names of leaders in local and national government, in media and entertainment, in education and business and the church. You will learn how to plug into sources that inform you of current national issues and local concerns. The church will keep you abreast of the world, targeting the least-evangelized areas on the planet, particularly the 10/40 Window,[29] and will give you models of letters for you to send to leaders to let them know you are praying for them.

Don't miss this marvelous opportunity to keep informed, especially if you have a prayer group. The church will also share other dynamic intercession plans and resources with you. (For more information, see the resources section of this book.) All you need to do is ask . . . and then begin and continue to intercede.

Thinking It Over

1. How do you feel about the plan for making the first Friday of every month a day of fasting and prayer for the church nationwide? Will you share it with your pastor or spiritual leader? Will you do it yourself?

2. Do you find the ideas of declaration and invocation exciting? Will you and your family, prayer group, and/or prayer partner put them into practice? Can you explain them clearly to others?

3. Is praying the television news a plan that would work in your home?

4. How do you feel about taking advantage of the Church on the Way's offer to share its wide-reaching praise and prayer plan?

Suggestions for Prayer

- Ask God to show you how to implement these intercessory plans in your own life and church.
- Ask God to raise up a massive intercessory army nationwide.
- Pray for a nation-shaking revival throughout the church in America.
- Ask God what you can do to be part of that awakening.
- Listen—and respond—to God's answer.

18

This Is Not the Time to Sleep

Years ago a musical called *Cabaret* came to our stages and screens. It is vulgar indeed, so please don't rush out and rent the video! But it is a powerful allegory. Much of the action takes place inside a cabaret in Germany during the beginnings of the Nazi movement. The cabaret patrons are a microcosm of prewar society, given over to a hedonistic pursuit of material, emotional, and sexual fulfillment. God doesn't even enter into the picture. Their philosophy is, "Eat, drink, and be merry, for tomorrow we die." Come to the cabaret!

Lions in the Street

While all the frenetic partying is going on and the empty relationships are building inside the cabaret, we have occasional flashes of what is happening just outside the doors: Young, arrogant, brown-shirted

193

storm troopers are strutting through the streets. They are only a small radical group. The cabaret performers make fun of them. The customers ignore them.

Gradually we glimpse the troopers' behavior becoming more aggressive as they begin to hassle the citizenry. Finally they start tormenting the Jews. Few in the cabaret take exception to this behavior or speak out. After all, it isn't their responsibility; why get involved?

Before long, however, these same brownshirts are filling the cabaret itself. Now they are the majority and can no longer be ignored. At that point it is too late to protest. The Nazis are in power. The party is over for everyone.

Likewise, if we don't wish to subject ourselves to the authority of the "children of disobedience" (see Eph. 2:2), we must do something about it now. If we don't pray for our government, use our courage and constitutional rights to make our voices heard for righteousness' sake, and exercise our blood-bought right to vote, the church may find herself with her mouth gagged and her hands tied. It is an ever present danger. We must not sleep during the seasons of seeming peace, because though the enemy may lie quietly, he only waits for us to close our eyes or leave our posts to play and he will be upon us. This is not paranoia; it is history.

We needn't constantly be looking over our shoulders or peering into dark corners. But we do need to be informed and to make prayer for our nation and its leaders a lifestyle, setting our faces for the long haul. Then we won't find ourselves in the position of desperately trying to deal with the consequences of what could have been prevented in the first place.

Had the church been awake, powerful in prayer, vital in her witness, and courageous in speaking out against unrighteousness in the name of the Lord, Nazism or communism or other tyrannous forms of government might never have reached their pinnacles of power. But because the church was either uninformed of her privileges in intercession or uninterested in exercising them, and because her witness was weak, the nations forgot God. The consequences were war and oppression.

Within those nations, however, a core of persevering intercessors continued to cry out. Gradually intercessors in other nations heard God's commission to stand in the gap on behalf of their brothers and sisters and joined the spiritual fray. As a result, we have seen despotic governments fall one by one. What if the cry had gone up before the despots were entrenched and the nations overcome?

The good news is that because of the understanding, faith, and perseverance of a few, God has again and again moved into the arena of national affairs. In the case of communism he blew down the walls with a suddenness that stunned the world. God may seem to move slowly, but when he moves, nothing can withstand him.

By Many or by Few

If your church isn't now practicing national intercession, have a talk with your pastor. If he doesn't catch the vision at first, go to your prayer group. Who knows? God may begin a powerful intercessory movement in your area if only you and one other person agree in determined and persistent prayer. The results may surprise you.

Look at King Saul and his band of six hundred men, with only two swords among them, as they face the Philistine army, which boasts thirty thousand chariots and six thousand horsemen. The armies are separated by a narrow pass between two rocky crags. So far no one has made a move.

While Saul's army rests in the camp, Jonathan, Saul's son, who possesses one of the two swords, decides to do something about the situation. He says to his young armor bearer, "Come on, let's go over to the garrison of these uncircumcised; it may be that the Lord will work for us; for there is nothing to prevent the Lord from saving by many or by few" (1 Sam. 14:6 ᴀʙ).

The Philistines see the two Israelites coming and shout, "Come on up here and we'll show you a thing or two!" Jonathan, having assurance that the Lord is with him, accepts the invitation, climbs up to meet the enemy, and slaughters about twenty men. The Philistines panic. The earth quakes and it becomes a terror from God. The Philistines turn their swords on one another in wild confusion.

When Saul and his napping army look across the pass into the enemy camp and see the fur flying, they finally realize what is happening and join the battle. Then the Israelites who have joined the Philistines turn back to fight for Israel. Even the Israelites who have hidden in the hills come out to fight when they hear that the Philistines are fleeing. And so God delivers Israel (see 1 Sam. 13:16–14:23).

Victory begins with only two brave men. Since in Old Testament typology Israel is a model of the church, we can picture from this story what can happen if a few Christians full of faith begin to attack the enemy:

- There will be casualties in the enemy's camp and panic in his ranks as he reacts in confusion to the unexpected attack.
- Many in God's sleeping army will awaken, see what is happening, and join the battle.

- Christians who have joined the enemy's camp will renew their allegiance to God's cause as it goes from victory to victory.

- Those who have been fearful and have hidden from the warfare will take heart and join the pursuit of the enemy.

Many people are waiting for someone to step out and lead the way. Without leadership, without vision, they will sleep on. Once you and a few "armor bearers" have begun the work, share your vision with churches and pastors other than your own. As pastors call their people to united intercession with others, you can stand together, an army raised up against the forces of darkness.

Remember, this is an ongoing war. When things look discouraging, don't stop praying. There should never be a time again when churches fail to make intercession for the nation a priority. We also pray that it will never become only a ritual but always be ministered with understanding and fervor.

We appeal to pastors to wake up your churches and teach them to become intercessors for the country. Remember, unless people have ongoing leadership and a structure to follow, few will long pursue a corporate effort. In appendixes A and B there are suggestions to help you begin and sustain an intercession ministry in your church and in your community.

Spread the Word!

If any or all of these intercessory efforts strike fire in your heart, please spread the message. Tell every Christian you know. Tell them about praying and fasting on the first Friday of the month, tell them about making daily invocations, tell them about praying the TV news.

Tell them about the Heal Our Land movement. Spread it on Christian radio, on television, in magazines, at conventions. Make life intercession a part of *your* life. Most of all, tell people about the saving, transforming power of Jesus. And tell your pastor about this book. Better yet, lend it or give it to him!

We call on pastors and worship leaders to implement these plans. As you teach them to your people, there will be intercessors all over our cities lifting their voices together from their homes, schools, and workplaces. Together we can make a powerful difference in our world as we literally shape the destiny of cities and nations through powerful intercession.

As an example of successful destiny-shaping, take the experience of Madras, Oregon. The Baghwan Rajhneesh, an Indian guru, and his devotees moved into that community and unobtrusively began buying up the town. Before the citizens woke up, the cult had managed to place people in significant positions of power within the local government and school system and pretty much ran the place. After they had established their position of control in the city, they began to hold mass free-love rallies, which included sexual perversion, and to offer free accommodations to like-minded people from all over the country. It became a terrible mess. By the time the press got wind of the goings-on and made it public knowledge nationwide, it seemed too late to change things.

However, the cult made some mistakes. First, they purchased a Christian church and used it for storage and trash disposal. Then they publicly announced that Jesus Christ had failed by dying on the cross. When that hit the papers, Mario Murillo read it, and it was just too much for him to swallow quietly. Immediately he had his crusade director contact the local Christian organizations in Madras and booked the local high school auditorium. Then Mario flew in to give a sermon titled "Did Jesus Fail by Dying on the Cross?"

The auditorium was packed. After preaching the gospel and leading a host of souls to Christ, Mario told the people that *now* was the time to stand and pray for their city in intense intercessory warfare and to keep on praying until the job was done. The Holy Spirit gave him three specific miracles to ask for:

- First, that someone of high rank in the cult would turn against the Baghwan and expose him.
- Next, that the Baghwan would incur a government investigation leading to criminal charges.
- Finally, that he would be deported.

They prayed that these miracles would be complete within six months. Almost to the day, these things came to pass in startling detail as the Baghwan's right-hand leader exposed him and caused irreparable damage to the organization. Then the unrelenting media assault forced state and federal investigations of cult activities, leading to indictments for fraud. And last, the Baghwan fled the country for India. The dump became a church again, and the properties were reclaimed by their original owners.

Mario says, "It was none of my doing that wrought this miracle. It was the army of God who took their rightful place of authority in prayer and, through intercession, literally recaptured their own community."

You don't have to let the devil devour your families or your communities. Don't lose the war by default. Stand up! Put on the armor. Pick up your weapons—and fight! Whether we are many or few, let us "wage war on the devil as though [we are] performing a dance," persevering with all confidence and joy.

God is listening—and it is *not* too late!

Thinking It Over

1. What can you do to spread the word about the Heal Our Land prayer strategies in your church and Christian community? Is it worth a concerted effort, perhaps a project spearheaded by your family, Sunday school class, or prayer group? Ask God to give you specific direction.

2. If you are reading this book in conjunction with a prayer partner or a Bible study/prayer group, recap and discuss what you've read, covering any areas you may not have had time for earlier.

Suggestions for Prayer

- Wait on the Lord and, under the leadership of the Holy Spirit, pray for America and her leadership.

Appendix A

Getting Down to the Nitty-Gritty

What's the best way to put all this together and make it work? Here are some guidelines to help you get off to a good start.

Getting Ready

1. Be sure you are a child of God. If you have the slightest doubt, skip to appendix C, "How to Become a Child of God," and take care of that before anything else. Then you will be ready to pray with faith and power.
2. Humble yourself before God. Do a quick pride check.
3. Confess and repent of any known sin.
4. Take care of any unforgiveness you need to release or restitution you need to make.
5. Reckon yourself dead to sin and alive to God through Jesus Christ your Lord (see Romans 6–8).
6. Put on the whole armor of God (see Eph. 6:10–20).
7. Build your faith through thanksgiving to God for his personal blessings to you.

8. Spend time in praise and worship and thus invoke the presence of God.
9. Submit your thoughts, opinions, and desires to God (see James 4:7).
10. Resist the enemy and forbid him to speak to you (see James 4:7).
11. Listen!
12. Pray.

Throughout the book we've given you sample prayers. Some short ones are integrated into the text; the longer ones at the end of certain chapters can be prayed a section at a time, incorporating your own words with ours to get you started. In addition you can

- use the following prayer list;
- pray the television news;
- make daily declaration and invocation;
- wait on God.

A Prayer List for National Intercession

1. *Sins of the nation:* Confess national sins, ask God for mercy and forgiveness.
2. *Government officials from national to local levels:* Pray for blessing and guidance for the godly, salvation—or removal and replacement—for the corrupt.
3. *Your city:* In Jeremiah 29 the captive Jews in Babylon were told to "occupy" in the midst of their enemies and were given prayer responsibility for their city. If Christians around the nation simply intercede for their own cities, we will saturate the entire country with prayer.

4. *Courts:* Pray for justice for *everyone;* ask for judges who will make decisions in line with God's will.
5. *The military:* Pray for wise leadership, strong Christian influence throughout the ranks, blessing and protection in battle.
6. *Law enforcement agencies:* Pray for salvation, wisdom, compassion, and protection for law officers.
7. *Abortion:* Ask for protection for the unborn; repent for our legalized "shedding of innocent blood;" ask for legislators who will fight abortion. Pray for compassionate, Christlike hearts; wisdom; strategy for action; and blessing from God for those who take public action in this arena.
8. *Immorality:* Oppose the legalization of immorality; ask God to pull down legislators who support sin and to raise up those who support godly principles.
9. *Violence:* Resist the violent spirits that stir up terrorists, anarchists, and street criminals in your city and nation.
10. *The media:* Ask for people of integrity and truth in reporting; resist pornography in all phases of media.[30]
11. *Arts and entertainment:* Pray against immoral, blasphemous, and occult influences that permeate these powerfully influential forces in our society.
12. *The economy:* Pray for business leaders, national and international banking concerns, and for trade unions; ask for righteous and wise leaders; bring them under the influence of the kingdom of God in prayer.[31]
13. *Schools:* Ask for more Christian teachers and officials in our school systems; speak in prayer and in public against moral corruption and occult influences in our schools; pray for higher academic achievement by our students.

14. *Families:* Intercede for your own, your neighbors', and those in your church. Pray for healed relationships, academic, spiritual, and moral motivation for children, salvation of the lost.
15. *Your church:* Pray for your fellow Christians and their needs; pray for your pastor—he needs your prayer support!
16. *Christians in other nations:* Pray for strength and deliverance for those under governments that deny them their religious, civil, and human rights.
17. *Areas of special need in other nations:* Pray about world economy and food shortages, wars, and human rights violations, using newscasts and newspapers as guidelines.
18. *The poor and hungry:* Pray as you would for yourself (fasting will help you identify with their hunger); give mercy ministries and inner-city missions the money you would have spent on food on the days you fast.
19. *Revival:* Pray for a great ingathering of the lost and a revival of vision and dedication to God within the church. (We see God at work in these areas already—we need more!)
20. *Principalities and powers:* Resist ungodly ruling spirits in your city and nation through intercession, spiritual warfare, and invocational declaration.
21. *Intercessors:* Ask God to raise up an army of intercessors nationwide.
22. *Souls:* Pray for national and world evangelization, for laborers for the harvest to complete the Great Commission.
23. *Ears to hear:* Ask the Holy Spirit to pray through you, and let him use you as his vessel for intercession:

We do not know what prayer to offer nor how to offer it worthily as we ought, but the Spirit Himself goes to meet our supplication and pleads in our behalf with unspeakable yearnings and groanings too deep for utterance. And He Who searches the hearts of men knows what is in the mind of the [Holy] Spirit [what His intent is], because the Spirit intercedes and pleads [before God] in behalf of the saints . . . in harmony with God's will.

Romans 8:26–27 AB

The Prayer Group

If you have been reading this book alone or with one other person, consider getting a prayer group started in which everyone involved can read and apply the principles you have learned here. If you are already working with a Bible study/prayer group as you read through *Heal Our Land*, try dividing your group time into two sections: discussion (using the subjects listed in the book) and prayer. Some areas of discussion may require more than one session to cover them adequately.

If your group is large, break it into smaller groups, no more than eight or ten people, giving everyone a chance to participate. Mix the groups at each meeting so all the group members can get acquainted. Encourage everyone to read the book and prepare for discussion at home.

Use the "Getting Ready" outline at the beginning of this appendix. Work through steps one through seven in either large or small groups. (We like to do steps eight through ten—submitting to God, resisting the enemy, listening and praying together—in the smaller group.) At first appoint a leader in each group to take the others through the preparatory steps. Later you'll do them as a matter of course and most anyone can lead.

Don't move hastily under the tyranny of small silences; after one person prays, let others add their petitions on the same subject before moving on. For instance, someone prays for an upcoming presidential decision. Another adds prayer for wisdom and direction for all the president's decisions. Someone else prays for his advisors, another for his protection, still another for his family. When nothing more is forthcoming on that subject, move on.

In the beginning the class leader may offer prayer subjects from the list in the book. As the group progresses, however, it is better for people to begin speaking for themselves. Structure the prayer times as loosely as possible. However, a few ground rules can be given up front and repeated often:

- Move small groups far enough apart that you're not distracted by one another.
- Keep prayers short, no more than about a dozen sentences. Each person may pray more than once, but keep each time short. This gives everybody a chance to pray.
- Don't shout! God isn't deaf. Don't destroy other people's focus on God by becoming the center of attention.
- Speak up! Keep your tone at a strong, conversational level. If you murmur or whisper, how are others going to hear and agree with you? You might as well be praying at home alone.

Group leader: Bring tactful correction, if necessary, but do it privately. To the experienced intercessor who prays too long, you might say, "You know, most of these people don't have your experience. You can cover all the bases, while they're just getting started. We want everyone to participate. Would you help me encourage them by keeping your prayers shorter? You can always take another turn if you feel the group has missed something important. It would be wonderful for you to keep things rolling with just a few pertinent sentences here and there." If that doesn't bring results the first time, say it again. Every few weeks, give a session over to the personal needs of those in the group. Everyone involved will benefit greatly.

Filling Up the Tank

As time goes by, your intercessory effort may need refueling. Please use the resources section in this book to find some dynamic teaching on prayer that will keep you and your group motivated and determined. Have an outside intercession teacher speak to your group, or to your whole church, every few weeks. This will give you a grasp of what God is doing nationally and internationally through his intercessors. Getting the big picture, including a world view, will give you new and greater prayer targets and keep you excited about praying.

As you listen patiently together for the Spirit to bring his thoughts into your heart, you'll grow sensitive to his voice. Then you will find him leading you into the highest level of intercession—intercession that is born in the heart of God.

Appendix B

A Word to Pastors and Leaders

Over many years of ministering and teaching in churches of every stripe and in many nations, we have acquired something of a bird's-eye view of what is going on in the church at large. We've seen the same wonderful results of unity and love, and the same spiritual blockades created by divisive mind-sets, over and over again. So we would like to make some suggestions that we hope will make a significant difference.

As a remedy for the divisions among church leadership, we'd like to suggest the practice that is being used with great success in many places and is a growing trend: a multiracial, multiethnic, monthly gathering of local church leaders. These visionary men and women are bringing about racial, cultural, and denominational unity in their communities. There are three main objectives to these fellowships:

1. The first is to give pastors and leaders a place to bond with their peers. This may bring some repentance and reconciliation among themselves, which would be a good model for their people.
2. The second is to monitor the needs of the community and strategize as to how the united church

can minister there. Love L.A., a multiracial coalition of Los Angeles pastors, and the Atlanta coalition, both of which we mentioned earlier in the book, are prime examples of groups already involved in this type of outreach.

3. The third is to have this become a unified pastoral intercessory prayer force for the community and the nation. Together they can then lead their churches into ongoing intercessory prayer. We suggest that on the first Friday of each month they hold a combined area-wide prayer meeting for America, led by various pastors, encouraging the observance of prayer and fasting for the nation.

These pastors' meetings may mean the sacrifice of some time and some pride and prejudice. It may require vulnerability and lowered defenses. We saw this happen in an amazing way at the time of the Summit Conference of Church Leaders in America. The leaders were from all across the denominational spectrum—mainline churches, evangelicals, Pentecostals, and Catholics. The diversity of doctrinal positions and worship practices represented was enormous. In addition, some of these leaders had been feuding for years.

We wondered how we were ever going to attain the unity we needed for effective strategy-and-intercession meetings. Obviously we needed someone special to open things up and break the ice. The person we had planned on canceled at the last minute. The only substitute available was not one we would have chosen. Although we liked him a lot, we feared he was too famous, charming, learned, and glamorous to bring a sense of humility into this crowd of "Very Important People."

Well, our substitute got up looking every inch the most successful of pastors. He walked to the podium, smiled a wavering, fast-fading smile, then lowered his head.

"Brothers," he said softly, "if I don't have a new touch from God, I can't go on. Please pray for me." He then began openly to share his journey into desperation. There was a moment of shocked silence. Then these men and women of God began to pray for a new touch from God—not only for him but for one another. They put their arms around each other's shoulders and prayed for forgiveness and reconciliation.

God's first requirement had been met: "If my people will humble themselves . . ." From that point on, God's agenda was fulfilled as he gave us strategy for calling the church to intercessory prayer nationwide.

It was a miracle. And we almost missed it!

It happened because of one man's true humility and desperate hunger for God. God can move just as powerfully in local communities if the leadership is as wise, humble, and open as this. As long as the basic tenets of the gospel are not violated, the church should be able to operate in cooperation and love. As leaders listen to each other with understanding instead of attempting to reinforce pet doctrines, not only might they actually learn something from one another but they will set the perfect example for their congregations.

Dealing with Doctrine

When our church in Van Nuys, California, was just starting out, we had a very small outreach to young people in our community. In contrast, the huge Baptist church down the street was overflowing with teenagers. One night our pastor attended a ball game at the local high school. As he looked around at the crowd, his heart cried out for the souls of the young people there, and he was full of frustration that our church had not yet begun to reach them for Christ. He says, "Suddenly I realized they *were* being reached—by another part of the body of Christ. I wanted to stand up and shout, 'Bless God for Van Nuys Baptist!'" The goal is souls, not jot-and-tittle doctrinal agreement. All of us, especially pastors, should recognize and honor the strengths and contributions of other ministries. Doctrine is important. We needn't pretend to agree with things we think are incorrect, but at the proper time and place we can discuss differences without hatred or harm if we do it in the unshakable fellowship of our family relationship in Jesus Christ. As we worship together and "do love," we disarm the enemy—and one another.

Of course, with all the good intentions in the world, things may not always go smoothly in these meetings. Someone may, out of excessive zeal for a pet doctrine, exuberantly try to railroad everyone else into his camp. This fellow is all enthusiasm; tact, sensitivity, and good timing are not part of his repertoire.

Then there are those with suspicious, militant spirits—so unlike the Spirit of the Lamb—who come in sniffing the air, every quill erect. Their ministries often are built largely on tearing down everything that differs from their own party line.

You all know some of these folks, we're sure. Try your best to "do love" to them, because no one will ever need it more. Besides that, it will build your character. Be careful also not to judge a whole fellowship or denomination negatively by the attitudes of a few people who are unwise or abrasive.

The enemy can divide you only where you allow him to. He works through unsanctified flesh, undisciplined mouths, and judgmental hearts.

Who are you to pass judgment on someone else's servant? Whether he stands or falls is his own Master's business; and *stand he will*, because his Master has power to enable him to stand. . . . You, sir, why do you pass judgment on your brother? And you, sir, why do you hold your brother in contempt? We shall all stand before God's tribunal.... Each of us will have to answer for himself. Let us therefore cease judging one another, but rather make this simple judgment: that no obstacle or stumbling-block be placed in a brother's way.... The kingdom of God is ... justice, peace, and joy, inspired by the Holy Spirit. *He who thus shows himself a servant of Christ is acceptable to God* and approved by men. Let us then pursue the things that make for peace and build up the common life.

Romans 14:4, 10, 12–13, 17–19 NEB, emphasis added

Maybe God would like a sign on the door at these pastors' meetings: "All swords must be checked at the door to be beaten into plowshares." As leaders come together in humility, eager to bless and serve one another, they will find that much of their distrust and many of their differences were groundless, generated by Satan, who fears a loving, united church more than anything. If we stand together, we will be stronger than the united forces of darkness. United leadership builds the church that wins the world.

We know you're busy. We can just hear you saying that with all your other responsibilities, you don't have time for such meetings. We'd like to suggest that you think over some priorities. No matter how large and busy your church is, its individual program isn't as important as the work of the body of Christ as a whole. Until each pastor's vision is enlarged to move with the body rather than as an independent unit, the church will remain weak and divided. Unity must begin with you, the pastors and leaders. The flocks won't come together without the leading of their shepherds.

"But," you say, "there aren't any such meetings in my community. Who will start them?"

How about you?

Appendix C

How to Become a Child of God

For many this will be elementary teaching, but for some it could be a revelation or perhaps a final resolution of your relationship with God. It is worth a page or two of spiritual review to make your foundation sure.

God's plan for our salvation springs from his undeserved but overflowing love for us. It is simple enough for a child to understand:

- We all have earned an eternal death penalty through our disobedience and sin.
- God's law requires the payment of the penalty.
- God's love already paid it.

"For the wages of sin is death, but the gift of God is eternal life in Christ Jesus our Lord" (Rom. 6:23). Jesus Christ, God's son, was born for this purpose: In his mercy God has revealed himself to us in a form we can comprehend and in a body suitable for sacrifice. He became a man so he could die and thus pay the penalty for our sins. Through his sacrifice we are offered forgiveness and eternal life. But you, like all of us, must personally receive this sacrifice—this Savior and his gift of life. When you do that, you become a child of God: "To all who did receive him, to those who have yielded him their allegiance, he gave the right to become children of God . . . the offspring of God himself" (John 1:12–13 NEB).

Our part in this transaction is to turn away from our sins, confess our need of forgiveness, and ask the Lord to save us. If this is your desire, your prayer can be simple, but it is still a kind of weighty, eternal wedding vow, something like this:

Lord Jesus, I'm truly sorry for all my sins, and I ask you to forgive me. Thank you for taking my punishment by dying in my place. I thankfully receive you as my Savior. Make my soul clean now by your divine power. I pledge my heart, my allegiance, and my obedience to you all the days of my life. Amen.

If you prayed that prayer, confirm your salvation by confessing Jesus publicly: "If you confess with your mouth, 'Jesus is Lord,' and believe in your heart that God raised him from the dead, you will be saved. For it is with your heart that you believe and are justified, and it is with your mouth that you confess and are saved" (Rom. 10:9–10 NIV).

In a way it is like getting married: We take our vows before God and others. We make our commitment to God and he makes his commitment to us. We have entered into an eternal covenant with him and he with us. Here is Jesus' vow: "All whom My Father gives (entrusts) to Me will come to Me; and the one who comes to Me I will most certainly not cast out *[I will never, no never, reject one of them who comes to Me]*" (John 6:37 AB, emphasis added).

Once this covenant commitment is made, the Holy Spirit begins to change us from the heart outward. If you have made this commitment to Christ, you will find yourself becoming a new person inside (see John 3:3;

2 Cor. 5:17). If you've ever wanted to start over, this is your chance! Being born again is as real and life-changing as being born the first time. Once you've done it, nothing will ever be the same. A new life—eternal life—begins.

Once you've made that commitment, ask God to lead you to a church in which you can be discipled and in which you will receive the sacraments, godly counsel, prayer, fellowship, and love.

Welcome to the family!

Resources

Evangelization of America
To network for the evangelization of America, contact:

Mission America, 901 East 78th Street, Minneapolis, MN 55420; (612) 853-1762

Government Representatives
For names of government representatives, order:

The U.S. Congress Handbook, P.O. Box 566, McLean, VA 22101; (703) 356-3572
State Legislative Guide, Christian Coalition, 227 Massachusetts Ave., N.E., Suite 101, Washington, D.C. 20002; (202) 547-3600

Heal Our Land Movement
For enquiries regarding the Heal Our Land movement, contact:

Heal Our Land, P.O. Box 3000, Garden Valley, TX 75771; (903) 882-6113 or Fax (903) 882-3311

Inner-City Life-Intercessors
To network with national inner-city life-intercessors, order:

Christian Community Development Association Membership Directory. 3848 W. Ogden Avenue, Chicago, IL 60623; (312) 762-0994 or Fax (312) 762-5772

Media Leaders

For names of leaders in media, order the pamphlet from:

Master Media, 330 N. Sixth Street, Suite 110, Redlands, CA 92374-3312

National Government Issues

For weekly information on national government issues, order:

The Pastor's Weekly Briefing, Focus on the Family, Fax (800) 232-6459

Legislative Facts Wire, Christian Coalition, Fax (202) 547-3600

For monthly information, order:

Intercessors for America First Friday Newsletter, (800) USA-PRAY

Prayer Ministries

To network with national prayer ministries, order:

The U.S. Prayer Directory. 7710-T Cherry Park Dr., Suite 224, Houston, TX 77095; (713) 855-1417 (Ask Eddie Smith, director of the U.S. Prayer Track, for some of his own prayer publications and others he may recommend.)

The Arsenal catalog. This is a clearinghouse and networking ministry for international prayer ministries, the resource arm of A.D. 2000's United Prayer Track, Dr. C. Peter Wagner, Chairman. (818) 577-7122 or Fax (818) 577-7160

Spiritual Leaders

For names of national and international spiritual leaders, ask:

The Church on the Way, Prayer Office, 14300 Sherman Way, Van Nuys, CA 91405-2499; (818) 779-8000

(NOTE: This updated info is coming from Helen Melahouris at Church on the Way.) *The Prayer, Praise and People Report* from the Church on the Way is produced on computer software called PageMaker 4.0. A file template of the bulletin is available on CompuServe (GO CIN: Church Connections, The Church On The Way Library) or America Online (Christianity Forum, Resource Center). Look for files titled "Prayer Template."

Author: Bob Anderson
CompuServe: 73003,3272
AOL Bobbarino

The Church on the Way will send you a complete packet of information simply for the asking.

Ministries

The following ministries have programs that are "transferable." They will be happy to share information with you if you send a letter, include a self-addressed, stamped envelope, or include some loose stamps to help them with their postage expenses, which are considerable.

Advent Industries, Ed Padley, Director, 220 Oberlin Rd., Elyria, OH 44035; (216) 284-0377 or Fax (216) 284-0388

Rev. LaVerne Campbell, 4331 45th Ave., Sacramento, CA 95824; (916) 422-6542

Fred Jordan Mission, Willie Jordan, Director, (818) 915-1981

Heal Our Land, Jimmy Owens, Director, P.O. Box 3000, Garden Valley, TX 75771; (903) 882-6113 or Fax (903) 882-3311

Impact America Tour, Youth with a Mission, Mark Anderson, Director, 2824 130th St., Frederick, WI 54837; (715) 327-8147 or Fax (715) 327-4550

Love, INC. c/o First Christian Church, 1720 W. 17th St., Santa Ana, CA 92706; (714) 252-1035 or Fax (714) 252-0846

Mario Murillo Ministries, P.O. Box 5027, San Ramon, CA 94583; (510) 820-5470 or Fax (510) 820-6151

Mission America, 901 East 78th St., Minneapolis, MN 55420; (612) 853-1762

The Nicky Cruz Outreach, P.O. Box 25070, Colorado Springs, CO 80936

Peacemakers, David Byerley and Rich Wilkerson, Co-founders, (800) 900-6770 or c/o Assemblies of God, Division of Home Missions, 1445 Booneville Ave., Springfield, MO 65802

Victory Outreach, Sonny Arguinzoni, Director, P.O. Box 2427, LaPuente, CA 91746; (818) 961-4910 or Fax (919) 961-7710

Vineyard Church, Duncan Ragsdale, Outreach Pastor, P.O. Box 7497, Houston, TX 77248; Fax (713) 869-7500

World Impact, Dr. Keith Phillips, Director, 2001 S. Vermont, Los Angeles, CA 90007; (213) 735-1137 or Fax (213) 735-2576

Recommended Books

Barton, David. *America: To Pray or Not to Pray* (1988) and *The Myth of Separation* (1992). Wallbuilders, P.O. Box 397, Aledo, TX 76008; (817) 441-6044. David Barton also has other excellent books. His three video tapes, *America's Godly Heritage, Spirit of the American Revolution,* and *Foundations of American Government,* are "musts"!

Bright, Bill. *The Coming Revival.* Orlando, Fla.: New Life Publications, 1995.

Bryant, David. *The Hope at Hand*. Grand Rapids: Baker, 1995.

Dawson, John. *Healing America's Wounds*. Ventura, Calif.: Regal, 1994.

DeMar, Gary. *America's Christian History: The Untold Story*. Atlanta: American Vision, 1995.

Federer, William J. *America's God and Country*. Coppell, Tex.: Fame Publishing, 1994.

LaHaye, Tim. *Faith of Our Founding Fathers*. Colorado Springs: Master Books, 1994.

Wagner, C. Peter. *Warfare Prayer*. Ventura, Calif.: Regal, 1992. Wagner also has other books on prayer.

Whitehead, David W. *The Second American Revolution*. Elgin, Ill.: David C. Cook, 1982.

We hope these resources will help you get started or keep you going in intercession that will transform America.

Sincerely,
Jimmy and Carol

Notes

1. Richard Frothingham, *The Rise of the Republic of the United States* (Boston: Little, Brown, 1872).

2. Charles Francis Adams, collector, *The Works of John Adams, Second President of the United States* (Boston: Little, Brown, 1854), volume X, 229.

3. *Griswold v. Connecticut,* U.S. Supreme Court, 1965.

4. Paul L. Ford, ed., *The Writings of Thomas Jefferson* (New York: G. P. Putnam's Sons, 1894), 8:310.

5. We are not implying that all Supreme Court justices are enemies of God. There are heroes among them. Recent decisions protect religious rights and restore some that were lost. We applaud those righteous decisions. Thank God, too, for the American Center for Law and Justice, whose members have been consistently arguing before the Supreme Court and other courts for the rights of believers, and winning.

6. Please read Tim LaHaye, *Faith of Our Founding Fathers* (Colorado Springs: Master, 1994).

7. *Stone v. Graham,* U.S. Supreme Court, 1980. For further information see David Barton, *The Myth of Separation* (Aledo, Tex.: Wallbuilders Press, 1992).

8. Newt Gingrich, Speaker of the House of Representatives.

9. U.S. Department of Education report, October 1993.

10. Shelter Partnership, a nonprofit organization working with two hundred homeless shelters.

11. *U.S. News and World Report,* February 10, 1997, cover story.

12. For further information see David Barton's and David Bryant's well-researched books (see the resources section of this book), which graphically document this decline.

13. Pastor Duncan Campbell's address is listed in the resources section

14. See the resources section for the address to order this directory.

15. Rev. LaVerne Campbell's address is listed in the resources section.

16. For information about Mission America, contact: Mission America, 901 East 78th St., Minneapolis, MN 55420; (612) 853-1762. For inquiries re-

garding the Heal Our Land movement, contact: Heal Our Land, P.O. Box 4600, Tyler, TX 75712; Phone or Fax (903) 882-6113.

17. In Old Testament times the people of God were all of one nationality, but now we are the church of Jesus Christ. We bear his name and are his holy nation within all nations (see Acts 15:14; Rom. 10:11–13; Gal. 3:26). If you're not really sure that you are one of those people called by God's name, please see appendix C: "How to Become a Child of God." This is the most important question you'll ever settle about your own identity.

18. We aren't implying that we can ignore sin in the lives of others. Galatians 6:1 says to correct and restore those who are overtaken in sin, but without any sense of superiority and with all gentleness; in other words, in love.

19. Derek Prince, *Shaping History through Prayer and Fasting* (Old Tappan, N.J.: Revell, 1973), 42.

20. C. Peter Wagner, *Warfare Prayer* (Ventura, Calif.: Regal, 1993), 57.

21. This truth of identification is so important that it deserves a book of its own; we have only touched the edges of it here. It is the scriptural way to victory over sin. See Andrew Murray's book *Covenants and Blessings* (Springdale, Pa.: Whitaker House, 1984). It will absolutely change your life!

22. Peter Beyerhaus, "Evangelism: Inviting into the Kingdom of Grace," *Christianity Today* (April 26, 1974).

23. Harold Lindsell, *The World, the Flesh, and the Devil* (Canon, 1973).

24. *Newsweek* (August 30, 1993).

25. Andrew Murray, *Covenants and Blessings* (Springdale, Pa.: Whitaker House, 1984).

26. Shepherd Bliss, "Humanist Psychology Reaches toward the Transcendent," *Yoga Journal*, September/October 1985. Quoted in Johanna Michaelsen, *Like Lambs to the Slaughter* (Eugene, Oreg.: Harvest House, 1989), 34.

27. Pope John Paul II, *Crossing the Threshold of Hope* (New York: Random House, 1994), 92.

28. Ibid., 93.

29. The 10/40 Window is a zone extending from West Africa through Asia between ten degrees and forty degrees north of the equator. It is the least evangelized area in the world. Most of the world's Hindus, Buddhists, and Muslims live there. It holds 84 percent of the world's truly impoverished people, 95 percent of whom have never had a chance to respond to the gospel.

30. For insight into the methods of the TV news media, read Frank Peretti's book *The Prophet* (Wheaton: Crossway Books/Good News Publishers, 1992).

31. For insights into this arena, see Pat Robertson's *The New World Order* (Dallas: Word, 1991).

Jimmy and Carol Owens are best known for their musical *If My People*. They are Christian musicians who have written many musicals for church use, including the adult musical *Come Together* and the children's musical *Ants'hillvania*. They are cochairpersons of the Worship and Arts Ministry Networks of both the A.D. 2000 and Beyond movement and Mission America. Their newest musical is *Heal Our Land*.